Scaling up Multiple Use Water Services

T0161502

Praise for this book

'This book provides a compelling argument for the water sector to look at MUS much more strategically, and for the growing number of local and community-driven development programmes to realize their potential in providing for the multiple basic needs around water services that poor communities grapple with across the developing world.'

Janmejay Singh, former Coordinator of the Community-Driven Development (CDD) Community of Practice, World Bank

'This book integrates what until now have remained separate, namely the drinking water and irrigation sub-sectors, despite more than two decades of efforts at alignment. The book provides a practical guide on how to overcome this artificial divide, and how investing in local water service provision can make a real difference for people, not only in terms of their health but also their wealth. This well-written book is not only a must-read for water engineers, local government planners, agricultural extension workers and public health officers, but also, and essentially, for politicians!'

Pieter van der Zaag, Professor of Water Resources Management, UNESCO-IHE Institute for Water Education, The Netherlands

'At last a book that tells us why MUS can both break down problematic silos in the water sector and provide multiple benefits to enhance human well-being. It also provides us with powerful lessons regarding scaling up and public sector accountability. This book is a must-read for anybody concerned with pro-poor and gender equitable water services and for solutions that emerge from the grounded experiences of local water users around the world.'

Lyla Mehta, Research Fellow, Institute of Development Studies, University of Sussex, UK

Scaling up Multiple Use Water Services
Accountability in the water sector

Barbara van Koppen, Stef Smits,
Cristina Rumbaitis del Rio and John B. Thomas

PRACTICAL ACTION
Publishing

Practical Action Publishing Ltd
The Schumacher Centre
Bourton on Dunsmore, Rugby,
Warwickshire CV23 9QZ, UK
www.practicalactionpublishing.org

ISBN 978-1-85339-829-2 Hardback
ISBN 978-1-85339-830-8 Paperback
ISBN 978-1-78044-829-9 Library Ebook
ISBN 978-1-78044-830-5 Ebook

A catalogue record for this book is available from the British Library.

van Koppen, B., Smits, S., Rumbaitis del Rio, C. and Thomas, J.B. (2014)
Scaling up Multiple Use Water Services: Accountability in the Water Sector,
Rugby, UK: Practical Action Publishing
<http://dx.doi.org/10.3362/9781780448299.000>.

Since 1974, Practical Action Publishing has published and disseminated
books and information in support of international development work
throughout the world. Practical Action Publishing is a trading name of
Practical Action Publishing Ltd (Company Reg. No. 1159018), the wholly
owned publishing company of Practical Action. Practical Action Publishing
trades only in support of its parent charity objectives and any profits
are covenanted back to Practical Action (Charity Reg. No. 247257,
Group VAT Registration No. 880 9924 76).

Cover design by Mercer Design
Typeset by Marie Doherty
Printed in India by Replika Press Pvt. Ltd

Contents

http://dx.doi.org/10.3362/9781780448299.000

About the authors

Dr Barbara van Koppen is Principal Researcher in Poverty, Gender and Water at the International Water Management Institute. She has 30 years of experience in action research and implementation of water services for multiple uses to poor women and men, and pro-poor water law in Africa, Asia and Latin America. She has written more than 80 international publications and is the co-ordinator of the MUS Group.

Stef Smits is Senior Programme Officer and Co-ordinator of the Latin America Regional Programme for IRC International Water and Sanitation Centre, based in The Hague. He has more than 10 years of experience in rural water supply, particularly in Latin America and Southern Africa. He has (co)authored various books and journal articles on rural water supplies, including on multiple use of water in such supplies, and is the secretary of the MUS Group.

Cristina Rumbaitis del Rio joined The Rockefeller Foundation in 2007. As a Senior Associate Director, Dr Rumbaitis del Rio has worked on initiatives related to climate change resilience in urban development, climate smart agriculture, water services delivery, and marine conservation and fishing. After receiving a doctoral degree in ecology from the University of Colorado, she became a post-doctoral fellow conducting research on sustainable development at Columbia University's Earth Institute. She has worked in Sri Lanka, Kenya, Ethiopia, India, Thailand and other countries.

John B. Thomas has been Program Associate at The Rockefeller Foundation since 2011. His work is focused on revaluing ecosystems, fisheries and aquaculture, water, and agricultural development. Before this, he worked on a project to develop innovative sanitation solutions that met the needs of Cambodia's rural poor through a partnership with the Hasso Plattner Institute of Design and International Development Enterprises – Cambodia (iDE). He has also worked in Kenya, Uganda and Namibia.

Preface

This book explores the links between global reform in public services towards accountability through local and community-driven development (LCDD) and trends towards more accountability in water services in rural and peri-urban areas in developing countries. The book's proposition is that the new approach of multiple use water services (MUS) is the pivot between the two. MUS is a public services approach that takes poor people's multiple water needs as the starting point for planning and providing water services. Since its emergence in the early 2000s, MUS has been tried out in 22 countries. Pilot projects and scaling up have taken place especially in a) the WASH sub-sector (as 'domestic-plus'), b) the irrigation sub-sector (as 'irrigation-plus'), c) the water sector without a pre-defined priority use (as 'MUS-by-design'), and d) implicitly in the new generation of multi-sectoral local and community-driven development (LCDD) programmes wherever communities prioritize improvements in water development and management (as 'implicit MUS').

This book uses the accountability triangle between citizens, policymakers and service providers and related concepts derived from global public services reform to analyse past pilot projects and scaling up of these four MUS modalities, and to recommend future steps. Evidence is mainly derived from MUS Scoping Studies in Ethiopia, Ghana, India, Nepal, and Tanzania; an MUS Roundtable supported by The Rockefeller Foundation, and from insights generated by over 200 case studies collected in the repository of the MUS Group. On this basis, the book develops three messages, one about the 'why' and two about the 'how' of scaling up MUS.

First the 'why'. MUS has five strengths because of the nature of water but they have been hidden in past service delivery because of the compartmentalization of the water sector into many sub-sectors. These strengths have been proven to lead to higher human development performance (or plausibly do). First, MUS leverages and supports water self-supply; self-supply is people's investment in water infrastructure creating the human, physical, technical, financial and institutional capital of local water development and management. Second, MUS follows people's priorities, so that services are owned and locally appropriate. Third, MUS generates multiple water uses and so multiple health and wealth benefits in people's multifaceted livelihoods. Fourth, MUS develops multipurpose infrastructure, which is more cost-effective as a rule; single-use infrastructure is the exception. Lastly, MUS efficiently considers the local water cycle and the use and re-use of its multiple sources.

The second message is about how to tap into these strengths, and the key changes required centrally by policymakers and managers of sub-sectoral water service provision organizations. They allocate funding and organize both the engineering expertise and the expertise to render water use more beneficial for ultimate health and wealth impacts, for example hygiene, agronomy, or marketing. Performance and job mandates are dominated by the expertise to create health and wealth through a single water use, although in reality performance tends to be measured as coverage, infrastructure construction, or production targets. Central-level MUS adopters have sharpened their performance to a goal of delivering water *services,* for multiple *uses* for human development *outcomes.* They also seek to make expert support more demand-driven and participatory, not just for a one-off project, but scaled up throughout their own and other sub-sectors. More horizontal communication between the water sub-sectors towards common goals for gender-equitable poverty alleviation would overcome current contradictions and ignorance between the sub-sectors. Such cross-sectoral goals could prioritize fund allocation and statutory water allocation to basic domestic uses and also to basic productive water uses by the poor. The latter is a domain for which neither the WASH nor the irrigation sub-sector (or other sub-sectors) took much responsibility in the past, despite international development goals and the socio-economic human rights frameworks.

The third message regards participatory planning at local level for the 'co-production of services'. This takes place in MUS-by-design projects and implicitly seems to emerge in LCDD projects in which communities prioritize water projects. The various pilot projects have contributed to the 'proof of concept' of MUS-by-design. This included initiatives for the market-led development and sale of affordable technologies for self-supply. To institutionalize participatory planning for MUS nationally, planning through local government is perfectly possible, provided local government is mature, as in India's National Rural Employment Guarantee Scheme, and central funding streams are available that are earmarked for the priorities set in the participatory planning process. Further research on the water components of these large-scale LCDD projects is expected to highlight how communities and local authorities have begun to tap into the five strengths of MUS and improve their performance.

These findings underpin the book's final recommendation to consolidate dialogue between global public services reform, MUS, and the water sector both in the continued piloting and scaling up of MUS and in in-depth comparative documentation, analysis, exchange, synthesis and advocacy.

Acknowledgements

This book is based on the experiences of innovating and scaling up of multiple use water services by a network of MUS champions, many of whom are core members of the MUS Group. Much of the conceptualization, practical implementation and change, evidence, and views presented here are the fruit of exchange and learning in the MUS Group. We gratefully acknowledge their contribution to the contents of this book.

The Rockefeller Foundation provided financial support to synthesize these experiences at country and global level, and to hold an MUS Roundtable at the Rockefeller Foundation's Bellagio Center – the most important steps in compiling this book. We thank The Rockefeller Foundation for this opportunity. We are also grateful for the financial support for this book from the International Water Management Institute and the Research Program on Water, Land and Ecosystems of the Consultative Group of International Agricultural Research.

Last but not least, we thank Sally Sutton and Jaap Bijl for their excellent comments on earlier drafts.

Acronyms

AWARD	Association for Water and Rural Development
CDD	community-driven development
CWP	Community Work Programme
INGO	international non-governmental organization
INWEPF	International Network for Water and Ecosystem in Paddy Fields
IWMI	International Water Management Institute
IWRM	integrated water resource management
LCDD	local and community-driven development
MG-NREGS	Mahatma Gandhi National Rural Employment Guarantee Scheme
MASSMUS	mapping systems and services for multiple uses
MDG	Millennium Development Goal
MUS	multiple use water services
NGO	non-governmental organization
O&OD	opportunities and obstacles to development
PAF	Poverty Alleviation Fund
RSA	Republic of South Africa
RVWRMP	Rural Village Water Resource Management Project
RWSN	Rural Water Supply Network
SDG	Sustainable Development Goal
TASAF	Tanzania Social Action Fund
WASH	water, sanitation and hygiene
WSP	World Bank Water and Sanitation Program
WUMP	water use master plan

CHAPTER 1
Rationale and aim

This chapter introduces the rationale of the book, which is a remarkable but hitherto ignored complementarity between the global reform in public services for more accountability to the poor and multiple use water services. The book's proposition is that strengthening these synergies will improve the water sector's performance in poverty alleviation and human development. The aim of the book is therefore to explore these synergies, based on the literature of public services reform as well as scoping studies and other documentation from more than a decade of piloting and scaling up of MUS across the world, in particular in the wash, sanitation and hygiene, and irrigation sub-sectors. The book's audience and structure are described.

Keywords: public services reform, accountability, WASH sub-sector, irrigation sub-sector, multiple use water services (MUS)

Rationale

In the past 10–15 years two approaches have emerged to improve public service delivery for gender-equitable poverty alleviation and human development: global public services reform in various sectors to strengthen accountability, and local and community-driven development (LCDD); and multiple use water services (MUS) in the water sector. Both approaches seek to reach the poor better and to meet their multifaceted needs. They place citizens centre stage as drivers of their own development and then strengthen service providers' accountability through citizens' empowerment and co-production of services. However, the existing and potential synergies between these two approaches have so far received little attention.

Worldwide public services reform covers many sectors, including the water, health, education, transport, and energy sectors. Communities and professionals from governments, non-governmental organizations (NGOs), and donor agencies collaborate with civil society, research centres, and the private sector to improve their performance by both strengthening accountability to the poor and innovating a new generation of poverty alleviation programmes (World Bank, 2004; Binswanger and Nguyen, 2005; De Regt, 2005; Binswanger-Mkhize et al., 2009; World Bank, 2011; Tembo, 2012). The decentralized co-production of services in these programmes has five pillars: the empowerment of communities; empowerment of local government; re-alignment of central government;

downward accountability; and capacity building (Binswanger-Mkhize et al., 2009). These approaches are widely recognized to improve performance in both poverty alleviation and human development, as well as in meeting the Millennium Development Goals (MDGs) and the new Sustainable Development Goals (SDGs). They also operationalize states' duties to respect, protect, and fulfil international human rights frameworks, in particular the socio-economic rights realized through public services.

Public service reform is changing water interventions in three ways. First, the LCDD approach has been applied to several water, sanitation and hygiene (WASH) programmes (De Regt, 2005; Binswanger-Mkhize et al., 2009; World Bank, 2011). Second, at a much larger scale, and possibly to the surprise of some water and development professionals, water components emerged in the rapidly growing multi-sectoral LCDD programmes wherever communities prioritized water interventions out of the range of options. This was the case at an unprecedented scale in India's Mahatma Gandhi National Rural Employment Guarantee Scheme (MG-NREGS). This scheme, which has been implemented nationwide through local government, provides minimum wage employment to over 50 million people each year. Communities and local government officials choose which assets are created with this labour. In two-thirds of all projects, communities prioritized water and drought-proofing assets, amounting to a total value of US$3 billion per year (Shah et al., 2010; Verma et al., 2011; Verma and Shah, 2012a, 2012b). Well over half of these assets were reported as being for multiple uses (Malik, 2011; Verma et al., 2011). Thus, by changing the programme set-up and decentralizing fund allocation to communities and local governments through well-designed community-driven planning processes, MG-NREGS became the world's largest rural water programme and, as we will show, the largest MUS programme.

Lastly, the water sector itself is also integrating elements of public services reform. For example, in both the WASH and irrigation sub-sectors, the focus is shifting from infrastructure construction (as output) to providing water *services* in the sense of water provision of agreed quantities and quality at agreed times and sites for people's actual use (as outcome). The management of public schemes becomes more participatory as well. Transparency International and the Water Integrity Network call for greater transparency and accountability in the water sector (WaterAid, 2006, 2008; WSP, 2010). There is also a growing recognition of people's own investments in infrastructure for self-supply. However, these shifts take place within many different water sub-sectors. The water sector is highly compartmentalized, with many sub-sectors that tend to focus on just one element of the hydrological cycle. This could be one water use, domestic use or irrigation but not both, or fisheries, or using only one source for the integrated physical water resources. This lack of horizontal co-ordination means that there is hardly any co-production of water services even within the water sector. As a result, people's water needs are, at best, only partially met. The sustainability of services and human development performance are both worse than they could be.

The other approach that has emerged since the early 2000s is MUS. MUS is a participatory, poverty-focused water services approach that takes people's multiple water needs as a starting point for planning and designing water services (Moriarty et al., 2004; van Koppen, 2006; Renwick et al., 2007). MUS focuses on people in rural and peri-urban areas with diverse agriculture-based livelihood strategies, the majority of whom are poor. They need water for many uses: drinking, other domestic uses such as washing, cooking and cleaning, livestock, (supplementary) irrigation, fisheries, tree growing, small-scale enterprise, crafts, and ceremonial uses. They are also very vulnerable to floods and other extreme events.

The MUS approach has been applied in 22 countries in Africa, Asia, and Latin America. The pilot projects revealed five partially proven and possible strengths of MUS for poverty alleviation and human development: leveraging self-supply; community ownership; locally appropriate priorities; multiple benefits from multipurpose infrastructure; and efficient management of multiple sources. Nevertheless, it appeared difficult to scale up the 'islands of success' and to institutionalize MUS into existing government structures in the water sector (Smits et al., 2010). The 'simple' intention to meet poor people's multiple water needs has far-reaching implications. People need a voice to express their multiple needs and priorities, while central agencies and authorities have to re-align to meet those needs, which are often well beyond the narrow mandate of their sub-sector. These are precisely the challenges of public services reform. MUS also aligns with the trend towards accountability in sub-sectors, but applies it *across* sub-sectors. MG-NREGS confirmed the potential benefits of water services reform to MUS: if communities and their authorities are given the opportunity and ownership, they often opt for leveraging self-supply and aim to get multiple benefits from multipurpose infrastructure, while considering the local water cycle in a holistic manner.

In sum, these two new development approaches are closely intertwined. Global reform in public services brings extensive experiences from worldwide piloting and scaling up in a range of sectors, along with robust generic synthesis and conceptualization. Moreover, it brings experience of innovative approaches for community participation in co-producing water services, and doing so at a large scale. MUS in turn brings insights in the specifics of water resources development and management and water's contribution to people's multifaceted livelihoods, in particular for the poor and women. MUS also brings empirical and conceptual lessons about potential and actual improvements in performance and about piloting and water sector reforms that already began in order to scale up accountability and decentralized co-production of services that meet poor people's multiple water needs.

Proposition, aim, methodology, and structure

This book proposes that further exploration of these synergies will open up new opportunities for governments, NGOs, donors, civil society and the private sector to improve public services performance for human development and poverty alleviation in water development and management in rural and peri-urban areas in developing countries.

It aims to explore the synergies between global public services reform and MUS and to identify both evidence-based and potential opportunities to improve the contribution of water interventions to gender-equitable poverty alleviation and human development.

This analysis is based on a literature review of public services reform with a focus on generic concepts and syntheses that also apply to the water sector as well as opportunities and obstacles to scaling up MUS. Much evidence on MUS piloting and scaling up comes from the MUS Group, a network that enables the exchange, learning, advocacy and synthesis of lessons learnt among its 14 international core partners and over 350 individual members. The repository of the MUS Group contains 200 case studies (MUS Group, 2013). This book builds on five national MUS scoping studies in particular, and their synthesis on the barriers to and potential for scaling up MUS. These scoping studies, conducted by the International Water Management Institute (IWMI) and the IRC International Water and Sanitation Centre and supported by The Rockefeller Foundation, are from India (Verma et al., 2011), Nepal (Basnet and van Koppen, 2011), Ethiopia (Butterworth et al., 2011), Ghana (Smits et al., 2011b), and Tanzania (van Koppen and Keraita, 2012) and are synthesized in van Koppen and Smits (2012). The analysis in this book also benefits from the MUS Roundtable in the Rockefeller Foundation's Bellagio Center in 2012, supported by The Rockefeller Foundation, in which global practitioners, researchers and policymakers involved in MUS took stock of past experiences to strategize on next steps (Ramaru and Hagmann, 2012).

MUS has been promoted most actively in a collaborative effort between the WASH and the irrigation sub-sectors, so this book will focus on those sectors, where most documentation originates. Evidence of MUS in other sub-sectors, such as fisheries and livestock, is scarce. Part of the analysis will be by logical conjecture. MUS is still too new for any ex-post evaluation and impact assessment. Moreover, monitoring and documentation of global public service delivery is weak in general, and MUS is no exception. In addition, the identification of promising solutions for better performance – the goal of this book – is intrinsically a matter of making a case, by conjecture, for the *design* of envisaged action that has yet to be implemented.

The book is structured as follows. In Chapter 2, we elaborate our proposition. We first present the insights from global public services reform that apply to the water sector in general and to the opportunities and obstacles faced in scaling up MUS in particular. We then move to the WASH and irrigation sub-sectors and assess their respective performances in alleviating poverty and bringing about gender-equitable human development, and their internal current trends towards more accountability to overcome weaknesses. We conclude with background information on MUS piloting and scaling up and show how MUS takes these trends forward within both sub-sectors (as the so-called 'domestic-plus' and 'irrigation-plus' MUS modalities), and increasingly also across the sub-sectors as the 'MUS-by-design' modality. We call water components that emerge from communities and their local authorities in LCDD approaches such as MG-NREGS the 'implicit MUS' modality.

Chapter 3 pulls evidence and conjecture together to outline the five reasons why MUS is bound to improve water services performance, and also explains why these five strengths have not been discovered earlier.

In Chapter 4, we present the lessons learnt from past efforts to scale up both +plus approaches to re-align services at central levels. These lessons unravel how the institutionalization of expertise in the sub-sectors defines single-use mandates and how a widening up of those mandates would allow a sub-sector to prioritize one use while also promoting other water uses. The chapter further unravels the objections to scaling up of MUS that we heard within both sub-sectors and that contradict and ignore the other sub-sector. A more consistent and mutually supportive cross-sectoral view on funding and water allocation priorities for pro-poor and gender-equitable water services is proposed.

Chapter 5 discusses the co-production of services in the overview of pilot projects of MUS-by-design. It analyses how hurdles were overcome but also the remaining challenges. Opportunities are explored for potential scaling up in the future through donors, implementing agencies, and local government.

Implicit MUS in MG-NREGS and other LCDD programmes that have already succeeded on a large scale are further examined in Chapter 6. This highlights how the institutional space for MUS can both be created and include opportunities for scaling up. We trace from the limited available information how this space is used and what challenges are left.

Conclusions and recommendations on action-research to further consolidate links between public services reform and MUS follow in Chapter 7.

Audience

We have written this book for professionals interested in public services reform, in particular around water, to highlight the promise these reforms hold for gender-equitable poverty alleviation and the fulfilment of socio-economic human rights and other internationally agreed goals. The book addresses fundamental policy questions to senior policymakers and programme managers in governments, donors and policy-relevant knowledge institutions. However, the book is also for the technicians, practitioners and extension workers on the ground who daily face the limitations of programme design in their efforts to make the changes in people's livelihoods successful. Their discretionary efforts to still meet their clients' multiple water needs despite their narrow top-down instructions were vital in triggering MUS innovation.

CHAPTER 2

At the crossroads of accountability in public services and multiple use water services

This chapter outlines the background of our proposition. We first present global public services reform with a focus on concepts and lessons that apply seamlessly to the water sector and will help in understanding the obstacles and opportunities for piloting and scaling up MUS, as discussed in later chapters. This is followed by an assessment of the current performance of both the WASH and irrigation sub-sectors and the partial measures that both sub-sectors have already taken to reach the poor and enhance accountability. The third section shows how MUS takes these trends forward across the sub-sectors. The section introduces MUS, its origins, and pilot projects from four different entry points or 'MUS modalities', and the scope of the scaling up of each of these modalities (domestic-plus, irrigation-plus, MUS-by-design, and implicit MUS). Documentation from these piloting and scaling-up experiences is the evidence base for the later chapters.

Keywords: accountability triangle, silos, co-production of services, self-supply, domestic-plus, irrigation-plus, MUS-by-design, implicit MUS

Public sector reform towards accountability for improved performance

The accountability triangle

The global knowledge base on accountability in public services entails many conceptual and empirical insights that are also relevant for the water sector and the remainder of this book. This section focuses on those. As an overarching framework, the World Bank (2004) conceptualizes accountability in services as a triangle between citizens (poor and non-poor), the state (politicians and policymakers) and service-provider organizations, within which instructions are given from the top down to the 'frontline' staff or local service provision officers who interact with citizens on a day-to-day basis (see Figure 2.1). In this triangle, relations in both directions are defined as accountable if: 1) there is a delegation of, or request for an expected service; 2) there are financial or other rewards for delivering that service; 3) the service is actually delivered; and

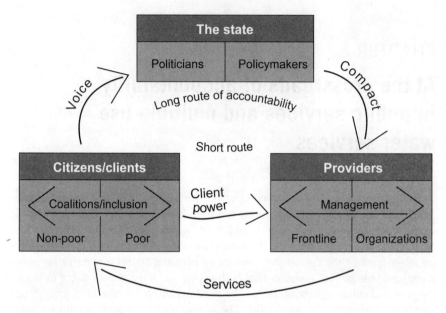

Figure 2.1 Triangle of service delivery and key relationships of power and accountability

Source: World Bank, 2004

4) the ability exists to enforce the expectation, which supposes; 5) that there is sufficient information about the service performance. A long and a short route to accountability are distinguished. The two sides of the triangle represent the long route to accountability, and the base is the short route.

The compact and 'silos' in the long route to accountability

The long route has two legs. First, citizens hold their politicians to account. In multi-party states this happens primarily through elections at local, regional and national levels, but also by lobbying, protest, and other forms of civil action. Citizens delegate an expectation of service delivery, for which many pay taxes. Citizens may be able to enforce their expectations in a next round of elections, provided they have sufficient information and reasonable promises of improvement in that next round. In the water sector, this leg can explain, for example, how the provision of drinking water or lowering of irrigation fees could help politicians to gain votes.

In the second leg, politicians liaise with the policymakers who set the rules and shape the organizational set-up that determines how those services are provided. Policymakers in turn engage with service-provider organizations, which are often government entities but can also be private or other providers such as community-based organizations, NGOs, utilities, or faith-based groups. The accountability relationships between policymakers and service providers are called a 'compact' (for state entities) or a 'contract' (for private entities). Compacts and contracts clarify performance agreements and rewards. Politicians and policymakers can enforce these contracts by maintaining or changing the service provider depending on its performance, at least if information on performance is available. Although a compact can be a clear contract, the compact is usually a broad agreement about a long-term relationship. It may specify the rewards (and possibly the penalties) for the service provider's actions and outputs, but this is not always as specific and legally enforceable as a contract. The frontline staff have to deliver the compact and have some level of autonomy or discretion, depending on the service in question. They have to reconcile their accountability upward to their superiors and their accountability downward to their clients in the short route to accountability.

In the compact, the administrative structuring of service delivery through higher level but separate sectors is also known as 'silos' (World Bank, 2004, 2011). Silos enable functional specialization and mobilize technical capacity. However, each silo sets priorities at the highest levels and monitors performance according to inputs and processes and, at best, sector-specific output indicators. These priorities often differ from local priorities, as the silos have a tendency to standardize priorities and not adjust for local contexts. In channelling resources from the top down, each silo follows its own procedures and timetables, creating major complexity on the ground. This hinders performance. Even professionals who fully acknowledge the need to combine several services for integrated, people-driven development admit at the same time that they see the delivery of elements other than their own as 'another department's problem' (World Bank, 2011: 39). Obviously, technical and specialist expertise is needed, so the challenge is integrating specialist expertise from one silo with specialist expertise of another silo, and with communities' knowledge, according to communities' priorities. Silos also occur in the private sector. Organizational development science has coined the term of the 'functional silo syndrome' to describe companies where different functions in the company (such as manufacturing, sales, or legal affairs) become isolated and a tall hierarchy develops in each one, to such an extent that they become incapable of reciprocal operation with other related systems (Ensor, 1988; AME, 1988). The sectoral set-up certainly applies to the water sector with its many sub-sectors that often operate in isolation in strongly hierarchical structures. In Chapter 4 we will discuss the stifling nature of these silos and how MUS innovation can overcome this.

Co-production in the short route and in the decentralized long route to accountability: LCDD

The short route to accountability is in the direct interaction between service providers and citizens. Citizens' voice is manifest as client power. Client payments for water services, vouchers or other contributions hold service providers accountable. Report cards, public spending tracking surveys and complaint procedures also reinforce client power. The ability to choose from among various service providers is crucial to enforce client expectations vis-à-vis the service provider and a major weakness in monopolistic service provision. In water services, clients can have this choice by investing in self-supply. In self-supply, or 'local' or 'private' water development, citizens invest in infrastructure construction, operation, maintenance and rehabilitation. This is largely self-financed and for their own use. People become their own service provider. Private-sector supply chains of water equipment and services increasingly support such self-supply. Obviously, when there are no public services self-supply is the only option.

Clients can have more choice in the short route to accountability when they become 'co-producers' of the service through participatory planning and implementation, a feature that we will discuss in Chapters 5 and 6 of this book. Co-production entails the empowerment of people, so the 'expansion of assets and capabilities of poor people to participate in, negotiate with, and hold accountable institutions that affect their lives' (Binswanger-Mkhize et al., 2009).

The World Bank and others have championed the community-driven development (CDD) approach since the early 2000s, building on earlier initiatives like the Social Grants. CDD often started as a separate 'enclave' approach, operating through implementing agencies in parallel to government structures. This enabled pilot testing of bottom-up, demand-driven and integrated approaches that are typically impossible within top-down compartmentalized government structures. The projects often aim at both development and employment creation, with either of these as the primary goal. In these projects, policymakers and donors provide national funding, which can be a pooled fund. Implementing agencies are tasked to support communities in the informed bottom-up planning of services, choosing from a menu of options, and these plans are funded and implemented. The inclusion of poor communities, and women and the marginalized within a community, is usually monitored by the systematic reporting of the wealth status and gender of project participants.

Such decentralized co-production of services strengthens accountability both in the short route to accountability (clients' prioritization of services) and in the first leg of the long route (holding local authorities accountable in their decisions over fund allocation). The second leg in the long route to accountability is considerably simplified, for example as guidelines, rapid approval procedures, village contracts, and social audits. Evidence is accumulating that such community-driven public services are more cost-effective and sustainable and have more livelihood impacts (World Bank, 2004, 2011; Binswanger and Nguyen, 2005; De Regt, 2005). CDD projects appeared especially successful for small infrastructure projects. Some CDD projects were WASH projects (De Regt, 2005).

Approaches by donors and implementing agencies, which have their own resources, are often appropriate for innovating and piloting integrated approaches, but they risk disappearing after project closure. Moreover, parallel initiatives can undermine government sovereignty and their own service-provision capacity. Therefore, CDD approaches increasingly supported local government in 'local and community-driven development approaches' (LCDD). Importantly, the co-production of services also implies local-level co-ordination of the various sectors, such as roads and transport, energy, health, and education. This warrants the re-alignment of central line agencies.

In the past couple of years, LCDD projects have grown vastly, leading to the multiplication of 'several islands of success that have addressed a national development problem to cover as much territory and population as possible and appropriate' (Binswanger-Mkhize et al., 2009). Indonesia, for example, radically reformed its country-wide local government and service delivery framework accordingly (World Bank, 2004). LCDD 'harnesses social capital through empowerment and increases social capital through scaling up' through the five pillars of the empowerment of communities, empowerment of local government, re-alignment of central government, accountability downward, and capacity building (Binswanger-Mkhize et al., 2009).

Thus, the long and short routes to accountability are linked. Strongly warning against any silver bullet, the literature suggests that addressing both routes simultaneously is the most effective (World Bank, 2004).

Foreign aid, which also plays an important role in the water sector of many countries, brings additional accountability relationships from donors to their own constituencies and between recipient governments and donors. Both the World Bank (2004) and the Paris Declaration on Aid Effectiveness (OECD, 2008) underline that foreign aid should strengthen and support the national development strategies of the sovereign state or should not undermine them. Foreign aid should avoid creating parallel systems and procedures, for example for reporting or procurement, which demand high transaction costs for the fragmented array of projects. In practice, this means that solutions are sought in channelling aid as sector budget support and sector-wide approaches, certainly in countries with good governance. An important pillar of the Paris Declaration is mutual accountability, in which donor and recipient countries jointly take responsibility for development results, and commit to providing more accountability to citizens and parliament for these results.

The accountability triangle framework enables one to assess how actual relationships in any situation either contribute to, or hamper, service delivery, and how pro-poor performance can be improved. Common distortions are, for example, that efforts to scale up co-production of services come up against the powers of central government vis-à-vis local people and their authorities, resulting in slow progress at best. Also, manipulation of the electoral system and political favours at national, district, and local levels distort service provision. Service providers can also exert power over politicians, certainly if they finance election campaigns. Similarly, powerful construction contractors can get away with inflated budgets. Local service provision officers may abuse their discretionary powers. Last, but not least, power relations reinforce the marginalization of poor men and especially poor women. In the long route, poor groups have less political clout and politicians may not respond to their needs. In the short route, poor people generally have less money to spend on services, so providers are less likely to listen to them. Within communities, the male elite may capture public resources and dominate 'participatory' planning at the expense of the poor and women. At the same time, the delivery of sub-standard services hits the poor hardest as they tend to be more vulnerable and less able to create alternatives through self-supply.

Current performance and accountability in the water sub-sectors

WASH

This section sketches the current performance of poverty alleviation and human development outcomes as well as trends towards accountability in the WASH sub-sector. The WASH sub-sector's overarching policy intention – as was most recently made explicit in the proposal for the post-2015 sustainable development indicators (JMP, 2012) – is to serve everybody with access to sufficient amounts of safe water for drinking and other domestic uses and sanitation, and which is sufficiently accessible for residents. This universal coverage would replace the current ambition of reducing lack of access by half, as articulated by Millennium Development Goal (MDG) target 7c. This goal is also driven by the adoption of a human right to water and sanitation (UN General Assembly, 2010).

The sub-sector has several expected impacts, but arguably the main expectation is one of reducing morbidity and mortality through waterborne diseases, as improved water supply and sanitation would cut some of the main transmission routes of such diseases. Whereas many sub-sector documents also state expected impacts on the well-being and productiveness of users, referring for example to the reduced drudgery of women and girls in particular and girls' increased school attendance, these are considered additional side benefits, alongside the overall health impacts. This bias towards health is clear, for example, in a recent evidence paper by DFID (2013) which goes to great lengths to carry out a meta-analysis of evidence of all sorts of health impacts – and particularly diarrhoeal morbidity – of WASH intervention, whereas the 'non-health' impacts are covered in a few pages. The seminal work by Hutton and Haller (2004) and Hutton et al. (2007) goes further and examines in more detail several of the other non-health impacts (alongside the health ones) of access to improved WASH services – and assesses the costs and benefits of this – though notably does not include the productive uses of domestic water supplies. This bias towards preventive health is also reflected in the fact that WASH in many countries still falls under the ultimate authority of a health ministry (in several countries in Latin America) or public health engineering department (India).

Despite the stated expected impact on health, the sector rarely measures its performance in terms of, for example, reduced diarrhoeal morbidity, for the simple reason that it is notoriously difficult to monitor and attributions of changes in morbidity to WASH alone are impossible to make. Rather, the sector has been using outputs as a yardstick for its performance, for example the number of people provided with access to an improved water source, as reflected in the MDGs. By this measure, the performance of the WASH sub-sector is reasonable. The MDG target for water supply was reached five years ahead of the 2015 deadline. By the end of 2011, 89 per cent of the population had access to improved water supplies. Of those without access, 83 per cent (or 636 million people) live in rural areas. This means that rural water supply coverage currently stands at 81 per cent (WHO/UNICEF, 2013).

While such output measurement is relatively straightforward, it is increasingly recognized that this only provides part of the picture. Therefore there is a trend towards measuring outcomes (Schouten and Smits, 2014), that is the levels of service that people receive, for example as reflected in the proposals for the post-2015 sector goals (JMP, 2012). Service levels indicate the characteristics of the supply that people actually receive, for example in terms of water quality, quantity or accessibility to residents (Lockwood and Smits, 2011).

Using these indicators, the picture becomes more nuanced, as many services are sub-standard and unsustainable. An estimated one out of three handpumps in Sub-Saharan Africa does not work (RWSN Executive Steering Committee, 2010). Elsewhere, a similar percentage of schemes fail (World Bank, 2004; Lockwood and Smits, 2011). And even where systems do work, they provide sub-standard services, that is, they fail on one or more of the criteria of quality, quantity or accessibility. Surveys in several districts in Ghana (Adank et al., 2013), Burkina Faso (Pezon et al., 2013) and Uganda (Bey et al., 2014) found that only 10–30 per cent of water systems (both point sources and small piped schemes) provided a service that met all official standards. The NGO Improve International keeps track of all the 'sad stats' of failing and underperforming WASH services, and these figures reiterate the same points: about one in three systems fail altogether, and of the ones that do not fail, most fail to meet one or more service-level indicators (Improve International, 2012). Onda et al. (2012) have shown that many 'improved' sources still have significant water quality risks. If water quality is to be truly accounted for, coverage with safe water would only be 28 per cent rather than the current estimate of 89 per cent (Onda et al., 2012).

One reason for system failure and underperformance is the problem that most systems are installed by private contractors without much involvement of public service providers, so no one is left properly equipped for maintenance. However, the full reasons are manifold and complex, and have been the subject of many studies (Schouten and Moriarty, 2003; Harvey and Reed, 2006; Lockwood and Smits, 2011; Moriarty et al., 2013).

The WASH sub-sector is moving in various ways to more accountability to overcome these flaws. First, since the late 1990s client voices are being heard better through the 'demand-responsive approach' which has rapidly gained ground (World Bank, 1998) and seeks a better match between demand and supply. However, as Moriarty et al. (2013) argue, there are fundamental weaknesses in this approach. In many instances, users' demand is insufficient. Users typically want water that is accessible and of sufficient quantity, but have much less demand for safe water – which is, as seen above, a key part of the public health focus of the sub-sector. Other users may in fact want more than what is on offer: more water, closer to the homestead, but they are not offered the choice of a higher level of service. Last but not least, a key element of the demand-responsive approach, the upfront cash contribution of users to the initial investment, is in reality often not made, or – for all kinds of reasons – is set so low that it is no longer an expression of users' real demands. At the same time, upfront payment may be unaffordable for poor men and especially poor women. They are over-represented among the unserved because they cannot afford the tariffs charged for public water services and are most in need of public support. All in all, the scope is limited for users to express their demand and for that demand to be met. Users end up with services that are either above or below what they asked for, and as a result payment for services is limited, most of the time covering basic operation and maintenance costs, but rarely rehabilitation or replacement costs (Fonseca et al., 2013).

A second area in which the WASH sub-sector strengthens accountability is through support to community-based service providers. Community-based management remains the main service delivery model in rural areas. However, as has now been widely recognized, community-based management has limitations. Communities can manage their services to some extent, but there are always operation and maintenance issues that they cannot address on their own (Schouten and Moriarty, 2003; Harvey and Reed, 2006). As a result, there has been a trend towards support to service providers by the authorities. In the compact, the policymaker or 'service authority' keeps a role in oversight, co-ordination, regulation and monitoring to enforce their expectations vis-à-vis the service provider (Lockwood and Smits, 2011), and they organize ongoing support to the service providers, which they provide either directly or via a contracted entity, such as an NGO, utility or private actor (Smits et al., 2011a). In addition, more professionalized forms of management are arising in some rural areas, such as private operators or public utilities or combinations of the two that follow clearer performance indicators as captured in contracts between authorities and service providers (Lockwood and Smits, 2011). All of this helps in the observed trend towards a service delivery approach (Moriarty et al., 2013), under which the commitment is to provide clients with water at agreed service levels, through a service delivery model, consisting of defined service providers (typically community-based), with oversight and support roles left in the hands of the authority, typically local government. In theory, accountability relationships are crystallizing out. In practice, many problems remain, particularly where local governments are underfunded for their support and authority roles (Smits et al., 2011a).

Third, civil society organizations such as WaterAid and the Water Integrity Network are calling for more accountability and equity by strengthening citizens' voice and control over service provider performance, for example by introducing report cards and score cards, and exposing corruption and mismanagement (WaterAid, 2006, 2008; WSP, 2010). However, these have generally been focused on WASH in urban areas. Gónzalez de Asis et al. (2009) and Velleman (2010) also provide a number of approaches, tools and examples for strengthening accountability in the WASH sub-sector. Transparency International (2008) in its annual global corruption report highlights a number of ways to improve accountability within these as well as other water sub-sectors.

Lastly, a trend towards more accountability is the growing recognition and support for existing self-supply, in particular private household wells. Users choose to use wells or develop other water systems if public service providers are absent or underperform. This would increase pressure on the latter to improve their services and be held accountable for that. Pursuing better health outcomes through improved water services, WASH policymakers and service providers can support private investments in various ways, such as developing technology for private supplies, developing the technology supply chain, providing financing facilities, and ensuring an enabling policy environment (see Smits and Sutton, 2012). Support to private household wells can entail improved covers or linings and better lifting devices (e.g. Sutton, 2007; Smits and Sutton, 2012; Sutton et al., 2012). It is significant that some of the earliest papers on self-supply in the WASH sector highlighted how self-supply is often driven by users' desire to have water for multiple uses (Alberts and van der Zee, 2003; Sutton, 2004), an argument only made stronger in subsequent self-supply publications (Adank, 2006; Sutton, 2007).

Irrigation

The following assessment of the poverty alleviation performance and trends towards accountability in the irrigation sub-sector highlights different targeting practices but also trends similar to those in the WASH sub-sector. The irrigation and agricultural water management sub-sectors usually fall under agriculture departments or specialized irrigation agencies. Projects often work from central levels to farmers; decentralization is still rare and local government's roles are small.

The sub-sector aims to provide water for crops, conventionally in public schemes, for household and national food security, employment generation, and multiplier effects in forward and backward linkages, including export (Molden, 2007). Performance is measured in terms of outputs of total irrigated areas, yields per unit of land and per unit of water, total irrigated production and its monetary value. The proportion of the designed command area of public schemes that is actually irrigated can also be monitored. Data about how much of a country's total irrigation potential is met are rarer, but the FAO Aquastat database does include indicators such as the percentage of irrigable land that is actually irrigated (FAO, 2013).

However, these neutral terms hide differences among the irrigators. Those with more land appear to benefit disproportionately from irrigation services. Services tend to reach the not-so-poor and wealthier farmers. Hussain et al. (2006) showed how poverty alleviation impacts of public irrigation schemes in Asia are strongest in schemes with smaller plot sizes. Yet, farm size distribution and even numbers of farmers are rarely monitored. Gender indicators are missing even more often, and public irrigation support is biased to men, even in areas where women are important farm decision-makers and land title-holders (Meinzen-Dick and Zwarteveen, 1998; van Koppen, 2002).

Unlike the WASH sub-sector, there is no policy in the irrigation sub-sector that seeks to reach every farmer with public services for irrigation. Only a few government programmes and NGOs target the poor, for example by allocating irrigated plots to the land-poor, or by targeting homestead land which the land-poor can access as well. Some NGOs develop and disseminate affordable individual technologies such as treadle pumps, rope-and-washer pumps or low-cost tanks, which are intended either for irrigation or for multiple uses. Even these efforts only reach a minority. The large majority of poor farmers are unserved.

This lack of policies to reach poor farmers and the male bias also holds for other sub-sectors with productive water uses, such as livestock, fisheries, forestry, and small-scale enterprises. There is no 'public owner' as yet who takes responsibility to better meet the productive water needs of poor farmers in order to achieve the international human right to food, non-discrimination, and participation, as well as the MDGs and Sustainable Development Goals.

In addition to the sub-sector's weak performance in reaching the poor, the productivity of existing public irrigation schemes is sub-optimal. Many schemes are trapped in build-neglect-rebuild cycles. Despite continued public investment, command areas can even be shrinking, as reported in India (GoI, 2011; Shah, 2012). Cost recovery in public irrigation schemes, even just for operation, is often partial at best. Maintenance and rehabilitation require continued subsidies, otherwise schemes produce even less or collapse.

While there are no clear trends in the irrigation sub-sector to better reach the unserved, trends to improve the irrigation sub-sector's performance of existing irrigation schemes are similar to the WASH sub-sector. Instead of top-down supply-driven water allocation, irrigation agencies are also moving to the notion of water *services* and increasingly seek to provide water of an agreed quantity and quality at an agreed time to an agreed site (Malano and van Hofwegen, 1999). FAO's Mapping System and Services for Canal Operation Techniques approach (MASSCOTE) is an example of this change (Renault, 2010).

A second similar trend is the promotion of users' participation. Downward accountability has been an important goal of the transfer of scheme operation and maintenance to water user associations since the 1990s and various studies have been conducted on methods to improve accountability (Paul, 1994;

Merrey, 1996; van der Schans and Lempérière, 2006). However, in some cases, especially in Sub-Saharan Africa, sudden irrigation management transfer and withdrawal of state support, without considering the range of factors that need to be in place for self-managed irrigation, affected production and even led to scheme collapse (Shah et al., 2002). Irrigator communities, civil society and research organizations have also analysed the role of the irrigation bureaucracy since the 1980s (Shah, 2009). Improved accountability between irrigation agency staff and users is proposed as one of the strategies to revitalize irrigation in Asia (Mukherji et al., 2010). Outright corruption in top-down infrastructure projects is also being exposed (Venot et al., 2011).

Lastly, both among the served and unserved, researchers from the irrigation sub-sector have paid attention to self-supply for irrigation and other uses, and have documented the human, technical, financial, physical and institutional capital that these investments represent for the majority of irrigators who farm outside the public schemes. Communal farmer-managed gravity irrigation schemes and spate irrigation in mountainous areas have been well documented across the Andean regions, Nepal, and Central Asia and Sub-Saharan Africa (Yoder, 1994; Boelens et al., 1998; Roth et al., 2005; Sokile, 2005; Boelens et al., 2007; van Koppen et al., 2007; Mehari et al., 2007; Bolding et al., 2010; Komakech, 2013).

More recently, research has highlighted the dynamism of individual self-supply, especially groundwater irrigation, which took off in a huge way wherever affordable mechanized lifting devices and affordable energy were available in Asia (Shah, 2009) and increasingly also in Africa (Pavelic et al., 2013). Electrification has drastically changed landscapes. Even in irrigation schemes, many farmers have private pumps, benefiting from the groundwater recharge by canals. In Pakistan, 41 per cent of the area of public schemes is irrigated in this way. In India, over two-thirds of the irrigating farmers irrigated with private pumps by 2003 (NSSO, 2005, cited in Shah, 2009). In Bangladesh, this was 70 per cent in 2000 (Bangladesh Bureau of Statistics, 2000, cited in Shah, 2009). In India, Pakistan and Bangladesh together, public schemes cover 31.2 million hectares, whereas private groundwater irrigation covers significantly more: 53.6 million ha. The millions of small-scale irrigators achieve higher yields with their private groundwater pumps than their counterparts taking water from public canals (Shah, 2009).

While pumps in distant fields may mainly be used for irrigation only, investments in self-supply are normally for multiple uses. The cascading village tanks in southern India are ancient forms of communal self-supply for domestic, irrigation, forestry and livestock uses (Palanisami and Meinzen-Dick, 2001; Palanisami et al., 2011; Venot et al., 2012). Pastoralists have managed their wells for livestock and human consumption over large distances. Water from rivers and flash floods is captured and diverted to recharge groundwater, for irrigation and for other uses (Mehari et al., 2007). Communities build institutional capital to address competition among these multiple water uses. Local water-sharing arrangements emerged, for example the rotation schedules of gravity-flow systems over large stretches of a river that crosses many villages (Sokile, 2005; Komakech and van der Zaag, 2011). In response to the depletion of aquifers in Gujarat, India, a huge popular movement of groundwater recharge emerged (Shah, 2007).

In the past, most irrigation policymakers and implementers ignored self-supply or saw self-supply as inefficient and backward, and in need of improvement. Local physical, financial, institutional and technical capital has even been eroded as a result of interventions (Boelens et al., 1998; van Koppen, 2002; Roth et al., 2005; Lankford et al., 2007; Coward, 2008). However, the trend is growing to provide public support for the promotion of self-supply along the same lines as in the WASH sub-sector, for example by technology development, private sector technology supply chain development, financing facilities, and providing an enabling policy environment (for example by reducing import duties for irrigation equipment). More affordable technologies and pump-rental markets ensure a somewhat better inclusion of the poor in self-supply.

Limitations

The foregoing review illustrates both sub-sectors' mixed performance in gender-equitable poverty alleviation, especially for productive water uses.

The three sorts of steps taken towards more accountability have limitations. Although there is a shift from top-down construction of infrastructure and command-and-control water supply (as output) towards water services and actual uses (as outcome), professionals are only held accountable for the single use of their sub-sector, and not for the full range of their clients' water needs. Further, user participation is only promoted in existing schemes and for operation and maintenance. People still often have no choice in the design and planning of infrastructure. Yet, it is very difficult to redress any physical design limitations from the initial system design through accountability measures at a later stage. If a water system was designed to provide only a minimal amount of water, or of limited continuity or frequency of supply, accountability measures alone cannot provide more water or provide it more often. Moreover, if participation is primarily promoted to save costs for governments, communities are burdened with the operation and maintenance obligations of a scheme selected by others without any post-construction support. Such 'participation' is likely to fail.

Professionals' interest in self-supply remains biased to the sub-sector. Studies on self-supply and local water management and potential public support measures focus on the single use of their sub-sector, or they focus on the range of productive uses, but ignore domestic uses. Only very few studies look into the human, technical, financial, physical and institutional capital of aggregate self-supply. An exception to the latter is the study on co-operation and conflict in local water governance in Latin America, Africa and Asia (Ravnborg et al., 2012). This project confirmed that people with agriculture-based livelihoods combine multiple water sources for multiple uses, through multipurpose infrastructure as the rule, and single uses as the exception, at homestead, hamlet, village or higher aggregate scales. While it is one step to recognize that, the next step is to translate that into public services design.

MUS is the water services approach that takes the next steps by shifting accountability downward to citizens and seeking to meet their multiple water needs according to their priorities, both in existing schemes and from the planning stage onwards in new schemes or extensions. MUS supports and leverages integrated self-supply.

Piloting and scaling up MUS

This section gives a brief history of MUS innovation and the four different entry points for water services reform for more accountability. Each of the resulting MUS modalities with their different scaling pathways will be discussed in later chapters.

Since the 1980s, water professionals in both the WASH and irrigation sub-sectors have observed that infrastructure which had been designed for a specific single use was, in practice, also used for other non-planned uses. Domestic water supplies were used for livestock, homestead gardening, and small-scale enterprise. Similarly, irrigation schemes were used for many non-irrigation uses, often including drinking water. These users included both irrigators and landless, and other poor people who lacked access to irrigated land and alternative water sources. Initially, managers in both sub-sectors felt these unplanned uses could damage infrastructure, for example, cattle could trample canal ditches. They also felt these uses could disrupt the designed water allocation rules. For example, illegal high volume uses upstream in canals and pipes would deprive tail-enders. The sector's usual response vis-à-vis this unruly behaviour was negative. Such uses should stop.

However, some professionals started recognizing the legitimacy and value of the livelihood benefits of these unplanned uses. Moreover, irrigation professionals noticed that these non-irrigation uses could be the main benefits of irrigation investment for landless people and women. In the irrigation sub-sector, calculations were made of the value of domestic water uses, fisheries, livestock watering, and horticulture (see Yoder, 1983; Meinzen-Dick, 1997; Bakker et al., 1999; Renwick, 2001; van der Hoek et al., 2002; Nguyen-Khoa et al., 2005, Molle and Renwick, 2005; Boelee et al., 2007; FAO, 2010). Similarly, productive uses of domestic schemes started and continue to be evaluated (Moriarty et al., 2004; Pérez de Mendiguren Castresana, 2004; Naidoo et al., 2009; Noel et al., 2010; van Houweling et al., 2012).

In order to better realize these benefits and to avoid the negative impacts of unplanned uses, professionals in both sub-sectors started to explore methodologies for planning to accommodate such needs. By the early 2000s the name of 'MUS' emerged for this new intervention approach. Central to these methodologies are people's multiple water needs and their participation in the planning and provision of water services that meet their needs. The 'S' of MUS stands for 'services', and so for providing water of agreed quantity and quality at an agreed time at an agreed site. The service provider is held accountable for these outcomes, while users are expected to pay for the services, unless (partial) subsidies are ensured. The piloting started from different entry points in the water sector, either in the WASH sub-sector or in the irrigation sub-sector. This was followed in institutional settings without an existing top-down defined single use either within the water sector or in multi-sectoral LCDD projects in which communities choose from a broad range of possible interventions. The synthesis of the early piloting experiences led to a distinction of 'MUS modalities', which became increasingly robust. These MUS modalities were then scaled up in the sense of sustainably institutionalizing the modality at larger scales and thereby reaching more citizens with more significant human development impacts. The sectoral setting was the primary pathway for scaling up. Modalities were defined according to the question: 'who prioritizes which water use in deciding about investments in infrastructure hardware and software and water allocation?' In this way, the following modalities were distinguished: domestic-plus, irrigation-plus, MUS-by-design and implicit MUS. In practice, the boundaries are more fluid, of course.

The +plus approaches

The modalities that operate within a sub-sector are called a '+plus approach', a term coined in 2003 by Butterworth (Butterworth et al., 2011). In the +plus approaches, the public sub-sector agencies prioritize the single use of their mandates but also promote other uses. These modalities are scaled up by leveraging both the existing financing streams and the technical expertise of the sub-sectors, so by reforming the compact in the long route to accountability. Thus, in the **domestic-plus** modality, the public sector sets the priority for domestic uses, hence supplies are close to homesteads in residential areas; productive uses are also promoted and tend to be concentrated at and around homesteads and are often small-scale.

Accordingly, the domestic-plus approach is in essence the promotion of higher levels of service, or 'climbing the multiple use water ladder' (see Figure 2.2) to allow for backyard gardening, livestock and home-based industries. In largely unserved areas, as in most of Sub-Saharan Africa, domestic-plus roughly means doubling or tripling current supplies up to an intermediate-level MUS of 50–100 litres per capita per day (lpcd), of which at least 3–5 lpcd should be safe for drinking and cooking. Add-on devices can be implemented to allow for other uses such as cattle troughs. Gardens can also be communal. Strictly speaking, the goal to move to higher service levels can be pursued without referring to the facilitation of productive uses, even when the requirement that all water at those higher service levels should be safe for drinking would be maintained. However, the articulation of productive uses enables the fine-tuning of water quality needs and mobilizing factors, such as inputs, skills and markets that render water use more productive.

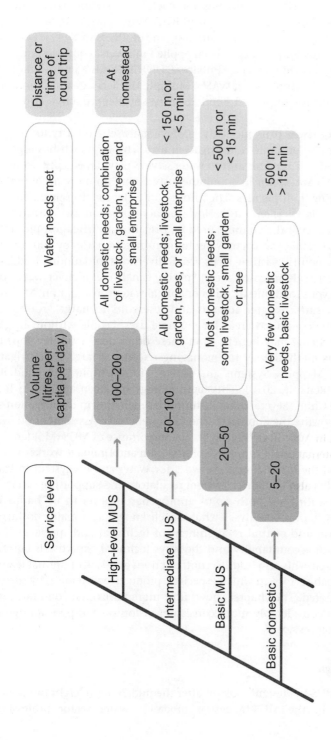

Figure 2.2 The domestic-plus water ladder

Source: Renwick et al., 2007; van Koppen et al., 2009

By now, an explicit domestic-plus approach has been applied in a number of programmes. For example, the World Bank Water and Sanitation Program promoted peri-urban homestead gardening in the 1990s in Kenya. Domestic-plus has implicitly and explicitly been applied in several countries, including Colombia, Nepal, Ethiopia, and Zimbabwe. UNICEF leads a multi-donor MUS project in Ethiopia (Integrating WASH, Multiple Use Services and Community Based Nutrition for Improved Food Security and Reproductive and Sexual Health).

In the **irrigation-plus** modality, professionals set a priority for irrigated cropping, but also promote non-irrigation uses. This approach has especially been promoted by FAO. The shift to water *services* plays an equally strong role as in the WASH sub-sector in simultaneously taking up more accountability and encouraging multiple uses. The priority for water for crops is maintained, but *not at the exclusion of other uses*. However, non-irrigation uses are often only a small proportion of the volumes used for irrigation, so irrigation-plus refers, in practice, to enabling access to water for non-irrigation uses by add-ons such as cattle entry points, washing steps, small diversions for laundry, bridges, or roads. In larger scale irrigated areas, specific canals may deliver water year-round to reservoirs for domestic water or animal water consumption. Moreover, seepage from surface water streams and reservoirs recharge groundwater throughout the command areas for multiple uses. People without irrigated land in the scheme may benefit from these other uses. FAO developed an irrigation-plus methodology for managing reforms of large-scale irrigation schemes, the Mapping Systems and Services for Multiple Uses Guidelines (MASSMUS) (Renault, 2010). This methodology has been applied in India, Vietnam, and China. Several other institutions originating in the irrigation sub-sector are following the approach. The Comprehensive Assessment on Water Management in Agriculture highlights the importance of MUS (Molden et al., 2007). The International Committee of Irrigation and Drainage works on MUS. Both FAO and the International Network for Water and Ecosystem in Paddy Fields (INWEPF) also include ecosystem regulatory and supporting services.

However, scaling up both +plus approaches appears to be happening only slowly. Chapter 4 analyses what is well known as a major obstacle to services reform and central re-alignment of technical and specialized sub-sectors: upward accountability and the ways technical expertise is currently institutionalized. This also leads to contradictions and lack of mutual learning between the sub-sectors, in which especially productive water uses by the poor risk being ignored. The chapter shows how more horizontal communication can lead to a considerably more consistent vision on pro-poor and gender equitable water services.

MUS-by-design

Piloting of 'MUS-by-design' took off after the mid-2000s in eight programmes or projects. In the MUS-by-design modality, water sector professionals set the goal of *water* interventions but without pre-defined priority uses or technologies. They leave this prioritization of investments and water allocation to communities through a participatory planning process. Self-supply is fully acknowledged in this co-production of services.

While these pilot projects came from different angles, they confirmed that, essentially, planning and providing services for people's multiple needs boils down to applying the steps of any participatory planning process to water development and management. This echoes the emphasis on empowerment of communities and local authorities in co-production of services through LCDD. The MUS Group synthesized these participatory planning steps and available tools into *Guidelines for Planning and Providing Multiple-use Water Services* (Adank et al., 2012), summarized in the following six steps:

1. introducing MUS to water users and service providers;
2. situational assessment (existing multiple uses, multipurpose infrastructure and sources of the local water cycle, especially by the poor and women);
3. visioning and strategic planning (including inclusive, transparent, informed prioritization of technology and institutional choices leading to a tentative workplan);
4. fitting the financial framework (transparent budget allocation to workplan at any level; negotiations of own contributions and local prices; mobilizing technical expertise);
5. implementation of MUS interventions (including transparent tendering and payments);
6. support for continuous service provision (post-construction support).

Chapter 5 presents the MUS-by-design projects and the different ways in which they operationalized such participation, and their current capability and potential for scaling up through the water sector.

Implicit MUS

In the 'implicit MUS' modality, the scaling up partners are the multi-sectoral LCDD programmes, in which communities decide about their priority intervention. The participatory planning processes in the co-production of services may, or may not, lead to opting for a water intervention. If they opt for water interventions, the institutional space allows them to meet their multiple water needs according to their priorities, so MUS is implicit. Chapter 6 traces evidence on what is happening in MG-NREGS and other programmes, as far as the very scarce documentation allows.

Table 2.1 summarizes the MUS modalities and their primary scaling up partners. These distinctions are analytical typologies. In reality, divisions are blurred and one modality can change into another. If communities prioritize water supplies at homesteads in MUS-by-design, it works out as domestic-plus. Or the +plus approaches may evolve into MUS-by-design, for example if the WASH sub-sector considers water supplies to wider spaces than homesteads and

Table 2.1 Overview of MUS modalities

MUS modality	Priority setting	Priority use and site	Technologies	Primary scaling up partners
Domestic-plus	WASH sub-sector	Domestic, near homesteads	Standard technologies and service levels, often communal	WASH sub-sector line agencies, NGOs, with local government
Irrigation-plus	Irrigation sub-sector	Single productive use, designated sites	Standard technologies, often communal	Agricultural line agencies, NGOs
MUS-by-design in water sector	Users, for water	Multiple uses and related sites	Technology choice	Implementing agencies, local government
Implicit MUS outside water sector	Users	Multiple uses and related sites	Technology choice	Implementing agencies, local government

residential areas. Irrigation-plus becomes MUS-by-design if domestic uses and homesteads are fully included. In situations where all domestic needs are met, MUS-by-design can become a productive–productive approach.

Conclusion

This chapter elaborated the crossroads of public services reform and MUS in order to corroborate our proposition that further synergies hold untapped opportunities for water interventions' contribution to gender-equitable poverty alleviation. Useful conceptualization and insights from global public services reform include the accountability triangle with its long and short route to accountability; the stifling nature of technical sectoral approaches; and the co-production of services, which promotes choice. We highlighted the need for reform in the WASH and irrigation sub-sectors as both struggle to deliver sustainable services. Moreover, the water sector's current performance in alleviating poverty and gender-equitable human development through small-scale productive uses is especially weak, and largely ignored by both sub-sectors. We also showed how both sub-sectors already adopted measures towards more accountability to overcome these weaknesses: they move to a services approach, to more participation and client's voice, and also increasingly recognize and support self-supply. The sketch of the history of MUS innovation and scaling up shows how MUS proponents have tried to take precisely these trends forward to meet people's multiple needs from the design phase onwards and across the sub-sectors. Piloting and scaling up of MUS has happened from within the sub-sectors (as 'domestic-plus' and 'irrigation-plus' modalities), increasingly without any pre-defined single water use and with some form of participatory planning and co-production of services, as the 'MUS-by-design' modality. LCDD approaches such as MG-NREGS provide a similar institutional space for community-driven interventions, and seem 'implicit MUS'. Efforts for scaling up MUS from these different entry points address different aspects of reform, as elaborated in the later chapters. Before that, Chapter 3 elaborates the core of our proposition: such reform opens up partly proven and partly plausible opportunities to improve the performance of water interventions for gender-equitable poverty alleviation and human development.

CHAPTER 3

The higher human development performance of MUS

This chapter elaborates the five strengths of MUS that are proven or plausible contributions to a higher human development performance: leveraging existing local capitals of self-supply; own priorities; multiple benefits; cost-effective multipurpose infrastructure; and efficient management of multiple sources.

Keywords: self-supply, ownership, multiple benefits, multipurpose infrastructure, multiple sources

The primary reason to further search for synergies between global public services reform and MUS in the water sector is the expectation that this can significantly improve the performance of water interventions for gender-equitable poverty alleviation. In the MUS literature, five reasons can be identified that corroborate this expectation, either based on evidence or based on conjecture. These strengths of MUS also underpin the launch of pilot projects, and efforts made in scaling up and advocacy.

Leveraging existing capitals

As indicated above, self-supply, in which people are their own service provider, is widespread and represents precious human, physical, technical, financial and institutional capital. Foster and Briceño-Garmendia (2010) indicate that about half of the capital investment in infrastructure used for domestic uses in Africa actually comes from users – much of it through self-supply. Similarly, even though a country like India has many large-scale public irrigation schemes, most irrigation is self-supply. This comes at no cost to the tax payer and widens people's choice vis-à-vis public service providers as well, leading to more power to hold them accountable. By taking existing water management arrangements as the starting point, MUS not only recognizes this capital and avoids destroying it (as has occurred in the past), but also leverages this capital. This comes typically at lower costs than any totally new scheme. Butterworth et al. (2013) indicate that, based on a rapid assessment of self-supply support programmes in Zambia, Zimbabwe and Uganda, for every dollar of public investment US$1.90 was leveraged in terms of household investments.

Own priorities

MUS enables people to decide how to allocate public financial, technical and institutional support and how to allocate water resources. This entails pro-actively providing information and support on options, but enabling people to decide on their priorities. This approach follows people's own visions on incremental improvements in water development and management, whether individually or collectively or both. This is not only at the heart of empowerment and accountability per se, but also increases the ownership and willingness to contribute own resources that are necessary conditions for the sustainability of public services. These performance improvements underpin global efforts to reform public services.

Own prioritization is particularly relevant for water interventions, not only because of the multiple domestic and productive uses, but also because of the strong local diversity in many relevant factors: geo-hydrology, weather and water availability, appropriate water technologies, and socio-economic and cultural contexts, and the related multiple opportunities and limitations to create more health and wealth with water. People oversee the broad range of their local opportunities and limitations. For example, they may prioritize rehabilitation over investments in any new infrastructure within given levels of funding. People consider options in a more holistic manner than professionals from compartmentalized water and other sub-sectors such as roads, energy, and markets. Having to handle this complexity would render specialists quite nervous. For people whose survival has depended on managing this complexity since time immemorial, it is their way of life (Mehta et al., 2001; Chambers, 2010; Rautanen et al., 2014). Thus, informed but own priorities are the bottom-up pull for integrated and demand-driven co-production of services by communities and service providers.

Multiple benefits

Unlike the single-use approaches, MUS seeks to achieve multiple uses and related human development impacts, including health, food, income, and reduced drudgery. The sum of these human development impacts is more than just the sum of each use and related livelihood benefits. Well-being is multifaceted. Better health boosts productivity. Income allows new investments in production and payment for domestic water and social services. Girls' time for school attendance better prepares them for the future and delays their marriage and child-bearing age, thereby reducing fertility rates. Similarly, vulnerability in just one dimension can mean falling back to extreme poverty. If women spend long hours fetching water for domestic uses, their productive activities, family care and rest suffer. As Renault (2010) coined it: MUS brings about 'most MDG per drop'.

Cost-effective multipurpose infrastructure

Multipurpose infrastructure is the most cost-effective way of providing water in almost all cases. As infrastructure is often the highest cost in water services, this feature of MUS is highly relevant. The cost-effectiveness of multipurpose infrastructure is reflected in urban water supplies, in which it is cheaper to have one distribution network with high drinking-water quality than having two distribution networks, one with high-quality water for drinking, and one with lower quality for other uses. Similarly, large-scale dams are typically planned for multiple water uses. The same has been proven in the WASH and irrigation sub-sectors.

One way of calculating this cost-effectiveness is in cases in which the non-planned uses neither cause significant damage nor disturb water allocation. Returns considerably increase simply by also counting the non-planned benefits, as was done, for example, by FAO (2010) in Figure 3.1. Calculating all returns is a stronger justification to make the investments and a broader basis for revenue collection.

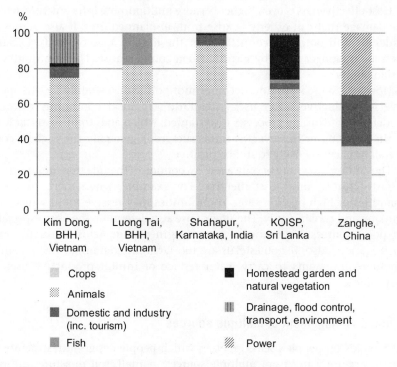

Figure 3.1 Share of benefits from various use of water in irrigation systems

Source: FAO, 2010

Another way of calculating cost-effectiveness of MUS is by calculating the incremental costs of converting single-use designs into multiple-use designs, and the incremental benefits that this provides. Single-use designs for domestic uses require, for example, larger pipes to bring more water to homesteads or the addition of cattle troughs. In irrigation schemes, additional cattle entry points, washing steps or provisions for year-round domestic supplies may be needed. The question is then whether such incremental costs generate sufficiently high incremental benefits to justify the additions for multiple uses. Various financial studies on this question have been done, especially for domestic-plus, and all found a very high benefit–cost ratio (Renwick et al., 2007; Adank et al., 2008; Hall, 2012). For example, increasing service levels for water supplies to homesteads from 20 lpcd to about 50–100 lpcd can be repaid from the extra income generated within six months to three years. Once basic domestic needs are met (approximately 20 lpcd), each additional lpcd generates an estimated US$0.50–1.00 per year of income (Renwick et al., 2007). Based on research in Senegal and Kenya, Hall (2012) calculated that users could repay capital costs of upgrading to intermediate-level MUS within one year for surface gravity-fed systems and around two years for groundwater pumped systems.

Cost-effectiveness is even higher because multipurpose infrastructure avoids the damage that can otherwise arise from unplanned uses. It also addresses trade-offs and potential conflicts from the design stage onwards, because users are no longer taken by surprise when conflicts arise. This contributes to sustainability.

However, standardization becomes more difficult, certainly for the more diverse productive water uses. Adaptation to local conditions through participatory planning processes is warranted, which adds to the costs, at least in the short term. However, as infrastructure is generally the highest cost, overall impacts are likely to still be positive.

The authors are aware of only a few exceptions to the rule that multipurpose infrastructure is most cost-effective. For example, when there are small quantities of high-quality water, communities may reserve those sources for drinking and cooking only. The sites of use also determine the uses, especially for point sources. Groundwater pumping in distant fields is usually only for irrigation. Also, if homesteads are too far from communal water points, labour requirements to carry water reduce or inhibit productive uses of that source.

Efficient management of multiple sources

MUS builds on people's self-supply, in which people design infrastructure to use and re-use water from multiple sources: rainfall, soil moisture, run-off, surface streams and reservoirs, wetlands, and groundwater. They tap into the natural and human-made local water cycle for more efficient use and re-use of multiple sources (de Lange and Penning de Vries, 2003). This starts at homestead level where households can combine up to nine different sources, as found in north-east Thailand (Penning de Vries and Ruaysoongnern, 2010). In and around command areas, people benefit from unlined irrigation canals that bring seepage water to their private household wells and groundwater irrigation pumps. Local people have considerable insight into their aquatic ecosystems and their links with other natural resources, contributing to, for example, flood protection, bio-waste breakdown, or storage of rainfall in groundwater and natural ponds. Quantity and quality of sources are adjusted to the uses. For example, protected household wells or rainwater tanks ensure safe water for drinking and cooking, while less clean water is used for purposes that do not require such high standards. This local knowledge and practice about ecosystems is an important contribution to public services (see Box 3.1).

Considering multiple sources opens up more and cheaper options that are environmentally more efficient than single-use services, which tend to focus on one source. Combining multiple water sources is also at the heart of people's coping strategies and resilience in the dry season and under extreme events. Considering the entire local water cycle opens up the potential to link water development and conservation when water resources become scarce. Local initiatives drove widespread groundwater recharge through wells, weirs and village tanks well before water conservation professionals started addressing these issues (Shah, 2007). These experiences corroborate the hypothesis that people for whom the sustainable availability of a resource is central to their survival are more committed than anyone else to manage and conserve their water sources as well as possible. Livelihood-enhancing measures are the main incentive for conservation.

Box 3.1 The overlap between public services and ecosystem services

The 'services' of 'public services' discussed in this book are profoundly different from the 'services' in 'ecosystem services', as defined, for example, by the Millennium Ecosystem Assessment (2005). However, they overlap in one important aspect. Public services are a necessary condition to realize ecosystem services. MUS is the most effective way to realize any aquatic ecosystem service.

The Millennium Ecosystem Assessment distinguishes four categories of ecosystem services: 1) regulation and 2) support services, which refer to the complex biophysical and chemical interactions between land, water and other natural resources; and 3) provisioning and 4) cultural services, which refer to the range of people's potential or factual domestic and productive *uses* of the natural resources and the related *values* of such uses in terms of, ultimately, human development. Many studies, including those by FAO and the International Network for Water and Ecosystem in Paddy Fields, have mapped and valued such actual and potential uses. MUS and water ecosystem services both focus on the full range of water uses and values for human development. MUS ensures that people's desired uses are sustainably realized, or that negative impacts (which could be called 'ecosystem dis-services') are prevented, through water infrastructure. In planning infrastructure, MUS taps people's own knowledge about water resources, such as their strategy to smartly combine multiple water sources. Accompanying measures (for example, hygiene education, markets) enhance the health and wealth benefits of the natural resource base.

Conclusion

MUS proponents have sought to empower communities, including beyond their sub-sectors. This has led to the discovery of five partially proven and partially plausible contributions to higher human development performance that, at best, had been only partially and unintentionally realized in the conventional sectoral water approaches. They reflect the unique nature of water resources and their development and management. These strengths are: 1) recognizing and leveraging self-supply, and 2) building upon communities' priorities and appropriate choices in complex situations, following communities' ways of managing water, 3) for multiple uses and benefits, through 4) cost-effective multipurpose infrastructure as the rule and single use as the exception, while 5) promoting the use and re-use of multiple sources in the local water cycle.

Achieving this higher performance requires drastic changes in the water sub-sectors from the central level downwards (as primarily pioneered in the +plus approaches) and to ensure participatory planning and co-production of services at local level (as pioneered primarily in the MUS-by-design and implicit MUS modalities). The next chapters present these lessons learnt and recommendations for further scaling up and action research.

CHAPTER 4

Scaling up the +plus approaches

This chapter presents the lessons learnt from efforts to scale up the +plus approaches from within their sub-sectors. The experiences are similar with regard to the same specialist hierarchical structure of sub-sectors, in which local service provision officers are accountable upward instead of downward to their clients. Jobs, fund allocation and the mobilization of technical expertise are determined at the central levels. The single water uses that are needed to create health or wealth, and the expertise needed to create those, dominate. The first section unravels how the +plus approaches seek to move to water services through functioning infrastructure, for multiple uses as human development outcomes. The second section discusses the contradictions of priorities for fund and water allocation between professionals of the two sub-sectors as a result of their single-use mindsets. We propose a horizontal conversation towards a common view on pro-poor and gender-equitable water services, which includes more attention to basic productive water uses for the large majority of smallholders outside public irrigation schemes.

Keywords: domestic-plus, irrigation-plus, mandates, silos, expertise, water services, human development outcomes, horizontal co-ordination, Nepal, South Africa, Tanzania

Widening the mandate of one's job

The most recurrent argument against scaling up of MUS and providing water for other uses than the single use of the sub-sector is that it is not seen as one's job. In the MASSMUS methodology, Renault (2010) gives a detailed description of this obstacle and also of the subsequent steps of sectoral professionals in adopting irrigation-plus. A similar process is found in the WASH sub-sector (Smits et al., 2010).

As Renault (2010) describes, the invariable wake-up call is the almost universal observation that infrastructure that was designed for a single use is, in reality, also used for non-planned uses. Commonly, the first reaction of professionals is to ignore or deny non-planned uses, or even try to prevent such 'illegal' uses, usually in vain. The next step is that professionals accept unplanned uses as a reality, but turn a blind eye, and say, 'not my job'. Then professionals start realizing how these non-planned uses generate livelihood benefits and returns on investments. This leads local-level staff to accommodate such uses on a case by case basis at their own discretion. The final step, which is to be taken at managerial levels, is planning and managing for the priority use of their sub-sector but also other uses: domestic-plus or irrigation-plus. Or managers may decide to leave any prioritization to communities in MUS-by-design.

The MUS Scoping Studies confirmed professionals' focus on only one water use as 'their job' and any other use as 'not their job'. A high-level Tanzanian irrigation policymaker realized how his engineers were 'livelihood engineers', but they should only accommodate such other uses 'on the way'. It should not affect their 'real' job (van Koppen and Keraita, 2012). In Nepal, an irrigation project manager put it clearly: 'The implementation of this irrigation programme is already so complicated we cannot complicate it even more' (Basnet and van Koppen, 2011). Thus, MUS is seen as something that competes in time and resources with their mandated work. How, then, is 'the job' defined in sub-sectors? What is this sense of competition and how can it be overcome? In the following section we develop a hypothesis of some of the contributing factors.

Defining job mandates at central levels

In our interviews, policymakers and even ministers, as well as most senior civil servants, in sub-sectoral line ministries often immediately appreciate MUS and the plausibility of its better human development outcomes. They also know communities' water management practices of meeting multiple water needs from multiple sources through multipurpose infrastructure, and they are aware of the unplanned uses in single-use designed schemes. Aware of their accountability to citizens (in the first leg of the long route to accountability), they are willing to provide integrated support. If such support goes straight from their highest levels to communities, this can be tailor-made. In Thailand, for example, high-level politicians directly supported the Farmer Wisdom Network in its campaigns to promote homestead-based livelihoods derived from multiple sources for multiple uses (van Koppen et al., 2009). However, for scaling up support to reach many more citizens, high-level policymakers need service provision organizations (in the second leg of the long route to accountability).

Professionals' jobs are defined in this compact between policymakers and the managers of service provision organizations. In setting up sub-sectors and allocating public resources for technical services, like water services, at these central levels, expertise plays an important role. Two types of expertise are needed. The first is hydrological and engineering expertise for infrastructure and water resources management and allocation, which can be assigned to rural engineering, public works or water departments. The second is expertise to make beneficial use of water in the fields of public health, sanitation and hygiene, agronomy, financing, or marketing. Measures to create more health and wealth accompany water investments. Water is only one of the inputs for health and wealth. This expertise for accompanying measures often plays a stronger role in designing governments' administrative organograms. For example, in Tanzania, a group of irrigation engineers moved from the Department of Agriculture to a new integrated Ministry of Water and Irrigation in 2008. However, the Department of Agriculture felt 'like an orphan', so in 2010 the irrigation engineers moved back to the then Ministry of Agriculture, Food and Cooperatives (van Koppen and Keraita, 2012). Foreign aid pooling of resources into national government budgets through basket funding tends to follow the silos. In Tanzania, one basket was for WASH, one for agriculture (with irrigation) and one for integrated water resources management. While such baskets reduce transactions costs and can lead to better targeting of investments in service delivery to the poor (de Kemp et al., 2011), they solidify the division in sub-sectors, even if a sub-sector is 'integrated' water management (van Koppen and Keraita, 2012).

This fragmentation of the water sector according to different single uses is reinforced by public vocational training and science and technology education institutions as a chicken-and-egg issue. Professionals have their own international journals and networks and promotion opportunities. Their professional ethos means they avoid stepping on each other's toes.

Further, policymakers and foreign aid organizations need to show human development impacts of water development in their accountability to voters and aid supporters. Appealing 'humanized' stories are important. Messages need to be simple in spite of the many factors that determine long-term human development impacts. Conventionally, human development impact messages also tend to be guided by specialized expertise to show how one water use leads to one dimension of well-being and via one clear pathway. Clean drinking water for health or smiling women farmers producing and selling shiny tomatoes are messages that are easy to convey.

Paradoxically, the valid concerns to ensure expertise and to achieve human development imply, in practice, that goals and performance indicators for the sub-sectors immediately jump to outcomes and ultimate human development impacts, but *only* for the outcomes and impacts that are facilitated by the experts employed in the sub-sector, and by water used for that purpose. Professionals in the WASH sub-sector promote health for all by reducing waterborne diseases through safe drinking water, hygiene and sanitation. They ignore health gains from other water-related pathways, such as improved nutrition, food or income. In contrast, the human development impacts that the irrigation engineers, agronomists and economists promote are food security and income, but only through cropping. Thus, legitimate and much-needed inputs by experts become counter-productive, and compound the power that the high-level managers of expert sub-sectors tend to exert in the competition for scarce public financial resources at central levels.

Lankford (2013) notes how specialists tend to argue with each other:

> Claiming to be interdisciplinary and good at running participatory workshops, when asked for solutions to address low-yielding resources,

people with well-developed career specialisms usually fall back on their training and 'office'. For example, 'price water' says the economist; 'breed higher yielding crops' says the biologist; 'line irrigation canals' intones the engineer; 'introduce new water laws' proposes the lawyer; 'form user groups' argues the social scientist, and 'partner with drip irrigation companies' suggests the policymaker interested in public–private partnerships.

Lankford proposes 'watereers' as 'professionals who would see the solution by looking at the resource via the eyes of a certain kind of resource user, and often those users who are least likely to represent themselves loudly at a resource workshop'.

Moving down the silos

Moving down the silos, the job mandates of lower level staff in recruitment and job descriptions, reporting requirements, reward systems, and promotion prospects reinforce the divides. Local staff members are held accountable for the single uses of their expertise-based sub-sectors, while others remain accountable for other uses according to their job mandates.

Efforts to strengthen accountability through expertise for human development become a paradox on the ground in several ways. As mentioned, human development impacts are claimed but rarely measured, among other reasons because of the complexity of measurement and attributing effects to causes. Performance indicators are generally based on inputs (funding, staffing) in relation to outputs (such as coverage of people reached and harvest per unit of land) and compliance with processes and procedures (World Bank, 2004).

However, in the water sub-sectors, even those inputs are rarely measured, although they are receiving more attention nowadays, at least in the WASH sub-sector. A relatively straightforward output indicator is the infrastructure constructed. So for the sake of accountability, quite detailed technical designs, unit costs, and bills of quantities are required in budget approval and tendering. Spending and construction are monitored (e.g. number of pumps, kilometres of pipes or canals) within given time frames and for a given budget. Thus, local service provision officers are held accountable and get paid and promoted by their superiors for implementing pre-set, already budgeted infrastructure outputs, as a take-it-or-leave it service, and *only* for the water use of his or her silo. They are discouraged from looking for any of the other water needs of their clients, for which they assume professionals in other silos are mandated. They focus on 'their' well-being dimension *to the exclusion* of other ways to meet that need and any other water needs of the same clients.

This implies limited co-production of services, as communities are not given a meaningful role, neither in the first development of the system nor in the ongoing service provision. Offering a choice to communities through a participatory planning process before construction or rehabilitation is tricky. It would not only delay tight implementation schedules but also risk identifying new needs and solutions that cannot be met within the available budgets already earmarked and monitored for single-use infrastructure. Pressure to spend money according to the top-down defined activities and timetables is strong. Returning unspent funds is seen as a sign of weak planning and management.

Local officers therefore have an incentive to carefully select communities and champions that are most likely to meet the performance indicators of their superiors. These are typically those who are most accessible and those with proven performance records, often the mostly male village elite. Local officers' upward accountability becomes an incentive for giving more to those who already have. This was the case in Tanzania. In allocating funding for new water supplies, district officials selected villages with a proven track record of sound financial management, which reinforced exclusion. This compounded the well-known phenomenon that the more dynamic and vocal ward councillors with more political and administrative connections find funds more easily. The haves get more (TAWASANET, 2009; Taylor, 2011).

The +plus approaches: services for human development outcomes

The domestic-plus and irrigation-plus approaches resolve various problems of these accountability paradoxes. They move towards a more meaningful output indicator: to water *services*, as a reflection of the sustainable functioning of the infrastructure to provide clients with water, and explicitly focus on providing water for additional uses, beyond the sub-sector's priority ones, and as prioritized by their clients. As sustainable water uses lead to sustainable livelihood benefits, water uses are essentially human development *outcomes*. The +plus approaches seek to promote these outcomes as their mandates in the performance agreements in the compact between policymakers and authorities and service provider organizations at central level, and in the communication messages to their respective constituencies. Broader human development outcomes are also rewarded in local and intermediate-level staff's performance evaluations. As mentioned, in quite a few cases local staff already started turning a blind eye on existing unplanned uses, or applying discretionary powers, for example in creative combinations of different funding streams (Mikhail and Yoder, 2008). The +plus approaches formalize and reward their local staff's human development outcomes.

To achieve human development *impacts* of health and wealth, expertise and accompanying measures remain vital. The challenge is to mobilize such health specialists or agronomists to provide such support according to demand in the co-production of services, instead of tying such expertise to one well-resourced project while most people remain without any support at all. In Tanzania, for example, most specialists report to both the District Executive Director and to their superiors in their line agencies. The District Executive Director can allocate staff as needed. Training and backstopping of cheaper, 'barefoot' technicians or health workers are important aspects of demand-driven and widely available expertise.

The hydrology and engineering experts in the .+plus approaches focus on developing appropriate technologies for multiple uses. In our experience, engineers may well welcome broader uses of their designs when this boosts adoption and functioning. The basic design principles that are taught in their professional education hold. Standing in for each other is already practised. For example, in the Mvomero District, Tanzania, we found that the district-level water supply and irrigation engineers take responsibility for any water infrastructure, depending on their availability (van Koppen and Keraita, 2012). The application of scarce engineering expertise is more cost-effective if it serves any water technology, instead of being confined to one sub-sector only. Solving the accountability paradox opens up more opportunities.

Horizontal co-ordination

In the past, local staff of service provider organizations were accountable upward. This gave hardly any incentive for horizontal co-ordination with colleagues in other sub-sectors, even if they were based in the same district offices. Their senior managers were perhaps even less motivated to engage in horizontal co-ordination, because these other sub-sectors were primarily competing for the same central funding streams of treasury and donors. The envisioned changes in performance indicators, accountability processes and one's job mandates also open up new possibilities, and even a need for more horizontal co-ordination for people who are 'water sector competent' in the technical specificities of water. We realized that during our interviews it was remarkable how discussions in the WASH sub-sector on the pros and cons of scaling up domestic-plus revealed objections that contradicted objections raised in discussions in the irrigation sub-sector on scaling up irrigation-plus. This not only suggests that the sub-sectors rarely communicate and learn from each other. It also shows how the compartmentalization into sub-sectors entails important, but hidden, decisions on the allocation of public funds and water resources in which professionals seem to compete, rather than collaborate. Because of the past lack of horizontal communication, these contradictions never came out. They can never be resolved within the silo set-up of the sector.

In this section, we list the topics of these objections, and the arguments heard in the WASH and irrigation sub-sectors respectively. The empirical evidence is still thin: we heard some arguments in a couple of interviews only. Nevertheless, the contradictions on each topic offer a basis to explore how these contradictions could be overcome 'beyond the silos'. Our proposals for consensus are meant to start a conversation in the water sector. In particular, they call for more attention to gender issues and the current lack of a public owner to support basic productive water uses, a field hitherto ignored, although

the Sustainable Development Goals and international human rights frameworks implicitly expect the water sector to play a key role in this respect.

Infrastructure fund allocation: a universal priority for basic domestic uses

The WASH sub-sector priority for public fund allocation to infrastructure for
everyone's access to safe water near the homestead and sanitation is widely
endorsed and aligns with many national goals, as well as the MDGs and human
rights frameworks. Most statutory water laws also stipulate a first priority to
water allocation for domestic uses. Even though reduction of drudgery for
women and girls is only a secondary goal, the mandate of improved domestic
water services aligns with the Convention of the Elimination of All Forms of
Discrimination Against Women of 1979, provided the service is affordable.

However, the irrigation sub-sector essentially ignores these national and
international public priorities and laws. If children and women have to draw
water from canals for lack of any alternatives, they can even forbid it.

Beyond silos, all water professionals would address basic domestic water
needs. Technical opportunities for synergies would be exploited, for example,
through adjacent wells that use seepage water from canals and reservoirs, or
piped diversions at the head where water is cleaner. Respecting this national
and international priority for basic domestic water supplies would be part of
the gender component of any irrigation service: the reduced drudgery also frees
up women's time that they can use for productive activities.

Water safety and health impacts: a universal priority for safe water for drinking

A common objection to domestic-plus by WASH professionals is that promoting drinking water for cattle and productive uses is 'wasting expensively
treated water'. Clients' water needs other than the WASH mandate are labelled
as a 'waste', even if users would pay higher tariffs for the additional use of
water, in the case of volumetric payments.

However, this argument misses the point that having parallel systems for
high-quality water for drinking and lower quality water for other uses would
often be even more expensive. It is for exactly that reason that hardly anybody
considers it a waste to use up to 100 lpcd of water of drinking quality for
laundry, cleaning or flushing toilets in urban areas – simply because running
parallel systems would be even more expensive. Being held accountable for safe
drinking water, the WASH sub-sector keeps placing extraordinary emphasis on
the highest water quality of *all* water provided, even though only part of that
water needs to meet these quality standards.

On the other hand, an irrigation professional in Nepal explained how
he genuinely felt accountable when he had to forbid people to drink water
from irrigation canals: 'If people drink this water and fall sick, I can be held

accountable'. Upward accountability leaves little incentive to recognize the problem and promote practical incremental improvements in clients' lives.

Beyond silos, it would be any water professional's job to contribute to improving the quality of water used for drinking, besides considering the need for reliable access to sufficient water quantities for hygiene and other domestic uses. Various practical ways exist to provide safe water for all:

- Accept that all water that is provided is safe, even if not all uses require that, just as is done in urban areas in Europe, for example.
- Provide parallel systems of high-quality and lower quality water for different uses.
- Promote point-of-use treatment. Within the WASH sub-sector much work is done to test and promote point-of-use treatment for the 3–5 lpcd that are needed for drinking and cooking (UNICEF/WHO, 2011). There is also scope for the unserved to apply point-of-use treatment, in case they have water sources close by that are of treatable quality. The urban middle-class in low- and middle-income countries solves the low-quality problem of piped supplies in the same way. However, education for sustainable uptake and hygienic uses is often still missing in poor areas.
- Promote other measures, such as spring protection, better hygiene practices around lifting and storing water, covering wells and other open storage facilities, recharging groundwater for well development, or tapping into more upstream water sources that are less polluted.

All of these options come at an incremental cost, though, an issue which will be addressed later in this chapter. In the same way pollution – for example from fertilizers and herbicides – would be everyone's concern.

Infrastructure fund allocation:
a universal priority for basic productive water uses

WASH professionals target, in principle, everybody. In the debates on the post-2015 Sustainable Development Goals, the option is raised to ensure that the rate of increase in access should be higher for poor families than for the non-poor. The thinking is that those with some level of access will need to continue receiving some subsidies to keep services running, particularly for capital maintenance, but this cannot be at the expense of increasing coverage to the unserved. The Joint Monitoring Programme has started making data available on levels of access of different wealth groups, highlighting the need to invest more for these groups. Given this goal, it is understandable that some WASH professionals objected to the adoption of domestic-plus approaches because they feared that domestic-plus would delay service delivery to the unserved, who do not even have access to water for basic domestic uses. Inequalities would widen.

It is true that domestic-plus services often require incremental initial investments which come on top of the already high costs of reaching the unserved in remote areas. Moreover, there will be incremental operational costs. Even in countries like France, the last households started to receive access to improved water supplies in the 1990s only, at huge per capita costs. In the meantime, service levels of citizens in urban areas gradually improved as well (Pezon, 1999).

The issue is that this argument ignores the legitimate productive water needs of the unserved. It also ignores the fact that it is often cheaper to provide multiple-use services from the outset, instead of first providing a basic level of service and climbing the ladder a few years later.

The irrigation sub-sector has no ambition to reach everybody with water services for productive uses and tends to be biased to male farmers with land, as mentioned above.

Beyond silos, all water professionals put poor people with multiple basic water needs centre stage. All water professionals would explore public services to meet basic irrigation needs (and basic water needs for livestock, forestry, fisheries, and other productive activities), in addition to basic domestic needs. The aim could also be to expand coverage in multiple basic water services of the poorest at a higher growth rate than those who have already been reached, or are able to invest in self-supply.

In many situations, the domestic-plus modality will be an appropriate way to operationalize this goal (Nielsen et al., 2006; Mikhail and Yoder, 2008; Basnet and van Koppen, 2011; Hall et al., 2013). Homestead-based productive water uses are particularly pro-poor and gender equitable. For the landless, the elderly and the ill, the homestead is often the only site where they can use water productively. Women's say over production at homesteads tends to be somewhat stronger than in fields, although this varies. However, especially in poor remote areas, there may be more cost-effective incremental improvements in local water development and management than universal domestic-plus. Inclusive participatory planning processes would reveal such options.

Cost recovery: potential payment for more uses

The most common argument for WASH professionals in favour of domestic-plus is that productive uses allow for income generation. This in turn enhances the ability to pay for services. Financial analyses have confirmed this potential, even for cross-subsidizing domestic uses with the incomes from productive uses (Renwick et al., 2007). Some evidence is emerging that there is a relationship between financial sustainability and the extent of domestic-plus (Hall, 2012). However, causes and effects remain unclear. Either people pay for services and ensure that systems perform well, which provides a secure environment for users to engage in productive activities. Or people started producing and generating more income to pay more for services. Or both processes take place and reinforce each other.

At the same time, the WASH sub-sector cautions that the emphasis on payment for services to recover part of the costs may lead to exclusion of the poorest. The less-poor have more funds to pay for services, and have other assets, so they tend to be more able and willing to pay, while payment for services remains unaffordable for the poor. Smart subsidy mechanisms should target those who are most excluded, but there is little experience as yet on how to do this.

Irrigation professionals also favour irrigation-plus because the resulting broader livelihood benefits give water users more incentives to pay for additional productive uses and domestic uses (Renault, 2010). However, despite the optimistic assumption of WASH professionals that the ability to pay increases cost recovery, the realities in public irrigation schemes provide little evidence that this is the case. Cost recovery is equally weak in both sub-sectors, so it remains to be seen how multiple use services can improve cost recovery. In both, the norm is that government pays the bulk of capital costs for infrastructure construction, and in practice for rehabilitation too. Irrigation departments sometimes even subsidize operation and maintenance. Or nobody pays in either sub-sector with scheme failure as a result. Politicians in both the WASH and irrigation sub-sectors risk their careers if they deviate from such subsidies (in the first leg of the long route to accountability).

Beyond silos, professionals would recognize that providing multiple use services *per se* widens the basis and stakes for payment and increases the ability and possibly the willingness to pay. However, more is needed to realize better cost recovery. Water professionals would jointly deepen analysis to develop cost recovery arrangements for water services. They would also ensure financing and subsidy arrangements to meet poor people's basic domestic and productive uses. Moreover, water professionals would also examine the broader features of MUS that are relevant for subsidy, financing, and cost recovery, such as the leveraging of existing capital; the ownership of public services if they address people's priorities for appropriate solutions; and the cost-effectiveness of multipurpose infrastructure and combinations of multiple sources. Moreover, cross-sectoral horizontal dialogue would identify and remove costly overlaps and promote convergence of public funding streams, while mobilizing different areas of expertise in a cost-effective manner.

Water allocation within schemes: universal priority for multiple basic water uses

Horizontal co-ordination would address not only fund allocation for infrastructure and water services, but also the allocation of water resources both within schemes (as discussed in this section) and at larger scales (in the following section). This would overcome the last set of contradictory objections to scaling up MUS that we found in the MUS Scoping studies.

Some WASH sub-sector professionals object to domestic-plus approaches because they fear that allowing for domestic-plus within their schemes 'will steal water designated for domestic uses away for productive uses'. Moreover, those with more land and other assets would use more water, which would further widen inequalities. The concerns to protect basic domestic uses and narrow inequalities are valid, certainly from the perspective of poor women. However, this argument ignores the fact that there are already productive uses in schemes designed for domestic uses. The fact that certain infrastructure is constructed with money from a WASH sub-sector's budget hardly affects villagers when they decide how they want to use the water. Even efforts to 'hardwire' certain priorities in the technical design are only partially effective, as was found in Nepal (see Box 4.1). Negotiations about water allocations are shaped by people's stakes and their complex, hierarchical relationships, often at the expense of the poor and women. Negotiations are also more influenced by the sites of water availability and upstream–downstream locations than by the technology in itself.

Box 4.1 Does the hardwiring of a priority for domestic uses work?

Winrock International and iDE in Nepal tried to hardwire a priority for domestic uses into their multipurpose piped gravity schemes by changing the common one-reservoir-one-distribution network into two separate reservoirs, each with its own distribution network. The engineers designated one reservoir and distribution network for domestic uses, while only the overflow of the domestic reservoir was channelled to another reservoir connected to a distribution network intended for irrigation. This works when homesteads and irrigated fields are located far from each other. However, when domestic water uses and productive uses take place around homesteads, people's multiple needs appeared to influence actual water use more strongly than the engineers' instructions that a specific off-take is designed for one specific use only (Mikhail and Yoder, 2008). In Bagargaun village, the Nepal MUS Scoping Study found that after the construction was finished, villagers retrofitted the design to the earlier model of one-reservoir-one-distribution-line. Instead of two taps around the homestead from two distribution networks linked to two nearby reservoirs, one bigger line has the same effect and is cheaper overall. The engineers realized that the best option was putting the issue of prioritizing water uses back into the hands of the community (Basnet and van Koppen, 2011).

In the irrigation sub-sector, we found a similar assumption that water conveyed by infrastructure that was funded by the irrigation sub-sector is, therefore, meant for irrigation. In the same piped gravity flow schemes in Nepal, it took long deliberations among irrigation officers before a pipe that was funded from an irrigation budget could be inserted in a multipurpose scheme that carried water which was also to be used for domestic uses (Mikhail and Yoder, 2008).

Nevertheless, irrigation professionals are not as worried as the WASH sub-sector about 'stealing' water for non-irrigation uses. In most cases, non-irrigation uses are all relatively small, if not negligible, compared to the water needs for crops. The irrigation sub-sector's concerns are about damage to infrastructure by unplanned uses. Possible competition with domestic water needs only arise, for example, when soap from laundry enters the canals, or when larger schemes that also supply water year-round for domestic uses and animal watering are interrupted for canal maintenance. At still larger scales, the increasing water needs of adjacent towns and cities can be the reason to adopt irrigation-plus approaches.

Beyond silos, water service providers would recognize water allocation as hardwired in the broader technology choice and its siting or layout, and as a continuous negotiation process between people thereafter. A priority for basic domestic uses would be supported by ensuring poor women's effective participation from the planning and design phases onwards. A priority for small-scale productive uses would require the strong voice of women and other marginalized groups in early planning and design. During the use phase, water professionals would facilitate the inevitable continued negotiations over water distribution, for example by enabling the setting of rules for such prioritization and their enforcement.

Quantification of the allocation issues shows that poor people's water uses are bound to remain small-scale because of the small size of homesteads and other land they may have, and the small scale of their enterprises. Even if many poor people would meet all conditions for the highest uptake of water (optimal skills, other inputs, rewarding markets), the total volumes of water used would often remain less than the luxury domestic uses of the non-poor, and certainly significantly less than irrigation uses of medium- and large-scale farmers. The real inequalities are among irrigators, so within the irrigation sub-sector rather than between the WASH and irrigation sub-sectors. The same principles hold at higher aggregate levels.

Water allocation at higher aggregate levels: a similar universal priority for multiple basic water uses

Moving up to higher aggregate levels, WASH professionals expressed a concern that universal domestic-plus may over-stretch available water resources. In the irrigation sub-sector no such concern was voiced. There is no issue in areas with economic water scarcity, that is where water resources are available, but infrastructure to use that water is lacking, as in most of Sub-Saharan Africa. The average total abstractions of renewable resources in Sub-Saharan Africa are estimated at 6 per cent (Bahri et al., 2010). Water resources are abundant but the means to develop them are limited, especially for the poor. This is also reflected in FAO Aquastat (2013) estimates of the significant gaps between actually irrigated land and the potential area that can be developed for irrigation given available land and water resources. Ethiopians irrigate an estimated 290,000 hectares out of the estimated potential of 2.7 million ha (FAO Aquastat, 2013). In Tanzania, out of 29.4 million ha of land suitable for irrigation, only 289,245 ha (1 per cent) was under formal irrigation by 2009/2010 (URT, 2009). Even in areas that are water scarce, irrigation policies keep expanding irrigated areas with no apparent concern about competing with the much smaller-scale domestic and domestic-plus volumes of water. For example, the Nepali government seeks to add over 400,000 ha to cover 80 per cent of its total area that is irrigable land by conventional means. Moreover, land around homes, which is considered unirrigable by conventional means, is targeted for piped systems and micro-irrigation (WECS, 2005). In areas of outright water scarcity, for example due to groundwater overdraft, the irrigation sub-sector's primary concern is about the competition for other irrigators and often less about the drying up of shallow wells that provide for domestic uses. The latter concern can be relegated to the WASH sub-sector.

Statutory laws usually define allocation issues by ranking sectors, typically with the highest priority for domestic uses, with agricultural, municipal or environmental uses in any next rank. This ignores intra-sector differences. Thus, high service levels for the urban middle-class of over 250 lpcd (to allow for lawn watering, for example) become legally a higher priority than the lower, minimum domestic *and* small-scale productive water needs of the rural population (Komakech et al., 2012a). The immense differences between the small- and large-scale irrigation or other uses are even more hidden. Thus, sector-based allocation depoliticizes water allocation at the expense of the rural and peri-urban poor whose basic productive water needs remain legally unprotected. The poor may even lose the tiny volumes of water that they currently use in locations with growing competition for water resources such as the land and water grabs by foreign investors since the late 2000s (Mehta et al., 2012).

Another bias against the poor in statutory laws in Latin America and Sub-Saharan Africa and increasingly in Asia is that they only recognize one legal system: administrative permit systems (Boelens et al., 1998; van Koppen et al., 2007). This implies that people's informal local governance over water development and management, including the capital and other strengths that are the starting point for MUS, are declared illegal. Under the erroneous assumption that one can change one legal system into another in the short term, every water user is either obliged to convert an existing entitlement into a permit or is exempted. Being exempted is a second-class entitlement leaving people without sufficient protection against permit holders. Permit applications in administration-based systems typically discriminate against poor men and certainly poor women. Thus, statutory law undermines basic entitlements promoted in human rights law (van Koppen et al., 2014).

Beyond single-use silos and sector-based water allocation, water is allocated to people with multiple water needs and not to sectors. The state's minimal duty is to protect everyone's basic domestic and productive uses enshrined in human rights. When water allocation becomes a zero-sum game, such protection implies a distributive reform that curtails water uses by the 'haves' to protect and expand water uses by the current 'have-nots'. Box 4.2 describes South Africa's inequalities in water use and water allocation policies and laws in this regard.

Box 4.2 Water allocation in South Africa

In rural South Africa, 1.2% of the population (largely commercial farmers) use 95% of the water resources. This equals a Gini coefficient of 0.99; where a Gini coefficient of 0 represents total equality and 1 total inequality (Cullis and van Koppen, 2008). Even if one more than doubled water use by all small users it would hardly affect the few large-scale users, according to hypothetical quantitative scenarios calculated for the Olifants Basin. In this basin, there are some 1,700 registered users and 290,000 unregistered rural households. The latter's current water use is estimated at 116 lpcd. The scenario was that they would increase their water uses up to 278 lpcd. This would provide 50 lpcd for domestic uses and 228 lpcd for a household irrigated plot of 1000 m² at 500 mm irrigation water per annum. (This is an unrealistically optimistic scenario because rural households lack the infrastructure to take up such volumes.) However, the projected implication for the 1,700 registered users was that they would have to share only 6% of their water uses. Alternatively, if only the ten largest users had to provide this extra water, they would have had to reduce their current water uses by 20% (Cullis and van Koppen, 2007). The impact of doubling or tripling WASH service levels to, for example, 100 lpcd for universal domestic-plus would be negligible, falling within the errors of the hydrological models.

South Africa's Second National Water Resource Strategy gives a high priority to water allocation for poverty alleviation and redressing inequities from the past. Only the Ecological and Basic (domestic) Human Needs Reserve and international obligations have a higher priority. National strategic uses for electricity generation and normal permit holders have a lower priority (DWA, 2013). However, it is still unclear how this priority will be operationalized and enforced.

Summary: re-aligning central goals

Table 4.1 summarizes what we have covered in this chapter so far. The first two columns list respondents' mandates. Their objections to (or support for) the corresponding +plus approaches that follow from their narrow mandates are presented in *italics*. If professionals stay within their silos, without horizontal communication, consensus is impossible at any level, especially to the detriment of poor people's small-scale productive water uses. Adopting the +plus approaches also warrants horizontal communication on how to remove current contradictions vis-à-vis their clients. Moving beyond silos opens up a conversation within the water sector as a whole on its responsibility as duty bearer to respect, protect and fulfil internationally agreed goals for which water is vital, especially for hitherto largely ignored small-scale productive uses.

Conclusions and recommendations for scaling up the +plus approaches

This chapter focused on the lessons learnt from discussions with sub-sector representatives at all levels on the scaling up of the +plus approaches. The topic of these discussions was the required changes at central levels in the negotiations between policymakers and senior managers of service provision organizations about the service providers' goals and performance indicators. The +plus approaches leverage the sub-sectors' available top-down funding streams

Table 4.1 Sub-sector objections against scaling up the +plus approach and potential common views

	WASH My sub-sector objects to domestic-plus because it is accountable to:	Irrigation My sub-sector objects to irrigation-plus because it is accountable to:	Potential common view Water professionals are jointly accountable to:
Human development impacts	Improve health through clean, nearby drinking water and sanitation. *Other ways to improve health and livelihoods are not my job.*	Improve food, productivity and income but only through crops. *Other ways to improve livelihoods are not my job.*	Meet multifaceted and mutually reinforcing livelihoods of all, with a priority for basic domestic and small-scale productive uses (e.g. as universal domestic-plus) Mobilize specialist expertise for livelihood impacts cost-effectively and on demand Mobilize engineering expertise for multipurpose infrastructure.
Water safety for health	Treat all domestic water, also for domestic uses that do not need drinking water quality. *Domestic-plus is a waste of expensive treated water.*	Forbid people to drink water from canals. *Drinking water quality is not my expertise and not my job.*	Ensure in the most efficient way that 3–5 litres per capita per day are safe for drinking and cooking Ensure larger quantities of water of lesser quality for personal hygiene and for other domestic uses, and for basic productive uses
Equity in fund allocation	Target basic domestic services to all to realize the human right to water for domestic uses. *Domestic-plus delays reaching the unserved and meeting their human right to water for domestic uses.*	Accept that providing more water to those with more land and other assets widens gaps in inequality. *Water to meet socio-economic human rights (food, livelihoods) is not my job.*	Ensure that all citizens, including the poor, have access to public funding for water infrastructure for basic domestic and productive water needs for all, smartly subsidizing the poor Tap the cost-effectiveness of MUS
Cost recovery	Cost recovery even for operation and maintenance is weak. *Domestic-plus generates income for better cost recovery (favouring domestic-plus)*	Cost recovery even for operation and maintenance is weak. *Irrigation-plus can generate income from non-irrigation uses for better cost recovery (favouring irrigation-plus)*	Broaden the uses and hence the basis for cost recovery Target subsidies to the poor for basic services Those who can pay should pay
Equity in water allocation within schemes and at higher aggregate levels	Infrastructure paid by the WASH sub-sector and designed for domestic uses means it is a priority. *Allowing for productive uses will steal water from domestic uses and increase inequities.*	Infrastructure paid by the irrigation sub-sector and designed for irrigation means it is a priority, irrespective of statutory and human rights law. *Domestic and livestock uses are negligible quantities, so acceptable if they don't damage.*	Prioritize water allocation for basic domestic and productive water uses for all Include women and other marginalized people in participatory planning from the outset to negotiate a priority for basic domestic and productive uses for all through technology choice and siting and rule setting

and technical expertise, but seek to render the accountability relationships and internal performance measurement arrangements stronger and more meaningful and better adapted to their clients' multiple water needs.

The +plus approaches propose to maintain the former single use of the sub-sector as the priority but to promote other uses as well. Such broader uses entail broader human development outcomes, which is positive. It tells a stronger human story.

For the monitoring of the construction goals in given time frames, the +plus approaches continue already existing trends to move beyond just construction, and measure their performance in terms of functioning schemes that sustainably deliver water services. The performance of implementing engineers and local staff is monitored more rigorously and meaningfully than when construction goals only were monitored. Engineering expertise from both sub-sectors can be pooled, instead of tying it to one project only. The incremental benefits–costs ratio for the incremental other uses is high.

The +plus approaches seek to end the situation in which expertise needed for the accompanying measures to transform water into more health and wealth dictate that only such single uses and the assumingly related human development impacts are defined as 'one's job'. Instead, such expertise should become more demand-driven and available for many more than just the beneficiaries of one particular project.

These changes that are likely to lead to more human development performance may seem neither too radical nor unfeasible. However, the experiences of a decade of trying to scale up the +plus approaches, including the interviews of the MUS Scoping Studies, showed that upward accountability in hierarchical sub-sectors is strong, and that horizontal communication has largely been absent. The tendency to defend the sub-sector's mandate instead of looking at communalities and new opportunities to deliver a better service together requires some give and take in a new conversation across the water sub-sectors around the specificities of water. Such conversation will soon have to open up to include sub-sectors beyond WASH, irrigation and water resource management and allocation.

All would recognize that their common clients are people with multiple water needs and that the poor who strongly depend on agriculture-based livelihoods are increasingly targeted for domestic uses but still ignored in their water needs for productive uses. We analysed in this chapter how the sub-sectors together can align with each other and ensure, first, a priority for water services for basic domestic uses, including 3–5 lpcd safe for drinking, *and* for basic small-scale productive uses; and, second, protection of these basic uses against competition by larger-scale users. Universal domestic-plus is a concrete operationalization of this goal and especially reaches women, the landless and sick.

We noted the importance of more formal discretionary power for local officers to accommodate diverse multiple uses, as some of them used to do informally in response to their clients' evident needs. This includes budgeting rules that allow various financing streams to be combined into integrated services. While central performance indicators for services and multiple uses of infrastructure are more meaningful and feasible, this alone does not remove the risk of top-down decision-making on infrastructure choice and expert support that is imposed on local officers and communities. As recognized in public services reform, improved accountability in the long route becomes more effective if accountability is also strengthened in the short route, through co-production of services by communities and the range of relevant sub-sectors (World Bank, 2004, 2011). For water interventions, such decentralization of funding and water allocation for co-production is MUS-by-design and implicit MUS. Their participatory planning processes enlarge the space to tap existing self-supply capital and ensure own priorities and ownership of multiple benefits, ample technology choice for multiple uses, and efficient management of multiple sources. The following two chapters discuss lessons learnt from piloting and scaling up MUS-by-design (Chapter 5) and implicit MUS (Chapter 6).

CHAPTER 5
Scaling up MUS-by-design

Eight organizations have innovated MUS-by-design and this chapter describes their experiences, as far as these experiences have been documented. The chapter starts with six organizations that are implementing agencies with donor funding. Coming from different angles, their approaches on planning and designing for multiple uses differ slightly. All provide proof of concept, but scaling up depends on the scope of the project and donor. The second section presents projects implemented through local government, one well-functioning project with its own funding, and another project that started the planning process with local government but failed to be implemented because funds were not mobilized by that local government.

Keywords: MUS-by-design, implementing agencies, local government, Ethiopia, Nepal, South Africa

In MUS-by-design programmes, multiple water uses (and human development outcomes) are the goal and performance indicator. Moreover, people set priorities in decentralized co-production of services through participatory planning processes or other forms of client power. Local staff and communities have access to financial support for priorities set in the participatory needs identification processes. Depending on their demands and in varying degrees, they can also access engineering expertise for infrastructure hardware and software, and expertise to turn water uses into more health and wealth. Clients' co-production of services enables them, in principle, to bring all their strengths, as described in Chapter 3, to the table. Unfortunately, information to test this is limited. These programmes are still recent and have not yet been documented, analysed and evaluated.

Scaling up MUS-by-design has also hardly been addressed yet, but we will derive some indications about the potential. Unlike the +plus approaches, which are scaled up by leveraging the resources of well-defined sub-sectors, the scaling up of MUS-by-design is more diverse and depends on both the entry point with related scaling partners and on the constellations of the projects. As mentioned, donor projects with independent implementing agencies are in general well equipped to pilot integrated approaches, but their sustainability and scaling up can be difficult. We will examine how this applies to the current experiences with MUS-by-design.

MUS-by-design is being implemented by eight sets of organizations in three constellations of service provision, namely:

- by donors with implementing agencies, including private sector involvement and promotion of self-supply;
- by donor-funded programmes implemented through local government;
- as capacity building in support of local government planning and implementation.

Table 5.1 gives an overview of the constellations and organizations and also notes the order of magnitude of clients reached.

Table 5.1 MUS-by-design projects in the water sector with approximate number of clients reached

Public sector constellations	Grants earmarked for water for multiple uses (estimated no. of clients reached since start)
Donors with implementing agencies	Technology NGOs (iDE, Mvuramanzi Trust, PumpAid, Connect International, etc.) (unknown)
	Africa/Asia USAID/Winrock MUS (250,000 since start)
	Catholic Relief Services, Plan International (unknown)
	SADC/Danida integrated water resource management Demonstration (1,000s since start)
	Women for Water Partnership (unknown)
	Ethiopia Community Management Projects (4,000 schemes for 2,000,000 users)
Local government programmes with state and/or donor funds	Nepal Rural Village Water Resource Management Project (796 schemes for 457,000 users)
Support to local government planning	South Africa Bushbuckridge MUS pilot (100s)

MUS-by-design through implementing agencies

Six organizations have pioneered MUS-by-design through own implementing agencies and with donor funds. While communities have a stronger voice in setting priority water uses in all cases, investments in infrastructure and the operationalization of 'participation' differed.

The first set of agencies consists of NGOs focusing on developing and scaling up technologies for multiple uses, often through market-led supply chains and support to self-supply. They target the poor who are able to pay. In the case of individual technologies, clients buy the technologies. Thus, innovation of rope-and-washer pumps has been ongoing since the early 2000s in Nicaragua (Alberts and van der Zee, 2004), and by Mvuramanzi Trust and PumpAid in Zimbabwe. iDE has innovated a range of affordable technologies, including plastic-lined homestead tanks, manual drilling, treadle and rope-and-washer pumps, and point-of-use treatment (van Koppen et al., 2009). RAIN Foundation promotes household biogas in Nepal and sand dams for multiple uses in Ethiopia. Connect International promotes an even wider range of low-cost individual technologies. While some initiatives originated in the WASH sub-sector, others came from an irrigation background, together making the point that, in practice, technologies meet multiple needs.

Winrock International

With its various partner organizations and supported by USAID and Coca Cola, Winrock International has pioneered the implementation of MUS-by-design since 2003. In Nepal, with iDE, 200 gravity-flow schemes for multiple uses have been implemented in collaboration with local government. Some scaling up took place through local government, other NGOs, and also through a special division of the Department of Irrigation (Mikhail and Yoder, 2008; Basnet and van Koppen, 2011). Winrock International continues expanding to other countries, including Tanzania, Niger, Burkina Faso, Mali, Rwanda, and India, with some 50 global staff working on MUS (Renwick, 2012).

The MUS Scoping Study in Tanzania highlighted Winrock's entry point in this country, which included setting up a market chain of locally produced, affordable technologies for water supplies for multiple uses, such as rope-and-washer pumps, treadle pumps, point-of-use treatment, and groundwater recharge. Local government appeared not particularly open to rope-and-washer pumps, which they initially labelled a 'dinosaur' technology. However, they later became more appreciative (van Koppen and Keraita, 2012).

Catholic Relief Services and PLAN International

In Ethiopia, Catholic Relief Services implements MUS-by-design as integrated catchment development and management, also reaching economies of scale. For example, four hamlets in the catchment of Adi Daero in Tigray were provided with a small reservoir, a canal with an irrigation scheme, and piped residential water. MUS activities by this NGO have expanded in Dire Dawa District (van Koppen et al., 2009). The INGO Plan International has followed similar approaches in Sri Lanka and Ghana, among other countries.

SADC/Danida

Danida supported the Southern Africa Development Community in designing and implementing integrated water resource management Demonstration Projects in six countries from 2006 to 2009. Implementing agencies in each country solicited selected communities' priorities for support for any aspect of water development and management. Priorities were diverse and included repair of small reservoirs and institutional strengthening; excavation of wells; spring protection; construction of a locally designed weir in a flood plain; gardens for 'outsiders' who had settled in a state scheme which was tightly controlled by a few founding co-operative members; electric pumps managed by elite households and to a limited (contested) extent opened up to neighbours; multipurpose manual pumps; and women's group petrol pumps. However, despite of the projects' long planning phase, funding availability tempted some implementing agencies and local elite to mainly serve the elite. In other cases, the implementing agencies negotiated intensively with the elite to allocate some of the benefits to the 'have-nots' (SADC/Danida, 2009a, 2009b). The German GIZ re-launched this approach in SADC with a consortium of national and European partners from 2012 onwards.

The Women for Water Partnership

The Women for Water Partnership is a worldwide strategic alliance of local, national and international women's organizations and networks. In a small grants project for water, The Women for Water Partnership empowered its grassroots members to translate their priority water needs into bankable proposals, typically for multiple uses – while many women prioritized domestic uses. The Partnership also linked its members to donors for these project proposals (Women for Water, n.d.).

Community Managed Projects

In Ethiopia, an innovative constellation known as Community Managed Projects emerged to rapidly and widely spread many simple water self-supply technologies. Although the project originated in the WASH sub-sector, the technologies were also used for production, which was encouraged. These projects are supported by the governments of Finland and Netherlands and UNICEF. They channel small amounts of donor funding through local micro-credit institutions to projects identified by communities. Local government facilitates information and technical approval, but communities keep funding in their savings accounts and decide about procurement and implementation. An evaluation of Community Managed Projects showed that spending and implementation rates of capital investments were five times higher than conventional projects (1,000 water points per year compared to 200 water points per year) with above average functionality rates (94 per cent using the approach compared to an average of 75 per cent). The budget spends were 100 per cent, compared to 53 per cent average for the WASH sector (Butterworth et al., 2011; CMPE, n.d.).

In sum, the experiences of the six organizations represent 'proof of concept' of the MUS-by-design modality. All organizations involve communities in the co-production of services. The contributions to infrastructure investment come from different angles, including integrated water resource management, affordable technology development, and financing for self-supply (assuming that technologies will be used for multiple purposes). Participation is a one-off process or an iterative learning process for agencies with a longer term presence, and can be targeted at women or other specific groups.

The collaboration with local government and line agencies varies. It can be limited to just mutual information, or government's national and local service provider officers are used and sometimes remunerated to select communities and to carry out and supervise project activities or provide technical support and quality control. Such relative autonomy and own funding allows piloting and building capacity in targeted communities and service providers. The integrated approach would have been difficult if not impossible to realize in the current compartmentalized government set-up.

However, the relative autonomy of implementing agencies implies that sustainability after project closure may be weak, unless the government partners are enabled to provide post-construction and other continued support, or sustainable market-led components have been set up. Also, without a long-term national scaling-up partner, the scaling up of this constellation requires continued contributions from donors. While donor interest in MUS-by-design is growing overall, other donors including Danida in Southern Africa have withdrawn.

The next two constellations are through local government. Do they fare better in terms of sustainability and scaling up?

MUS-by-design through local government

Rural Village Water Resource Management Project Nepal

The Rural Village Water Resource Management Project (RVWRMP), supported by the governments of Nepal and Finland, implements what we define as MUS-by-design through local government structures in 10 districts in the middle and far west of Nepal. Instead of working through implementing agencies, RVWRMP supports the statutory structures and planning and budgeting procedures of the Village Development Committees and District Development Committees, as well as government officials on the ground. Currently there is a Village Development Committee Secretary only, backed up by one or two technical staff. Because of the recent civil unrest there are as yet no locally elected councillors. The project fills this void by building community capacity for participatory planning. This prepares for future democratic structures (Rautanen et al., 2014). RVWRMP funds are earmarked to implement plans identified through these structures.

In 1999, well before the term 'MUS' was coined, staff of Helvetas, a Swiss development organization, were inspired by integrated water resource management and conceptualized their project approach as a water use master plan (WUMP). WUMPs align with the steps for MUS-by-design. RVWRMP adopted this approach in 2006 (RVWRMP, 2008). A WUMP entails an inventory of all water resources, technologies and uses, as also captured in GIS. Village Development Committees share their understanding on where the gaps are in various water resources and environment-related services and rank their priorities. Separate women-only or disadvantaged groups-only planning meetings are organized if their voices cannot otherwise be heard. The outcome of this methodology is a rolling, holistic five-year water development plan. In the current update of WUMPs, a WUMP is being split into modules that are less intensive and cost less, so they can be applied and replicated more widely (Basnet and van Koppen, 2011; Rautanen et al., 2014).

For the implementation of selected activities, Water Users Committees are established, registered and members extensively trained to plan, implement, oversee, operate and maintain their scheme. All stakeholders are guided by a step-by-step process that also guides the financial releases. When RVWRMP realized that micro-credit provision is pivotal in this region for access to capital and savings accounts, the project arranged for this accompanying measure (Rautanen et al., 2014).

One lesson learnt is that RVWRMP increasingly tapped benefits of multiple uses from multiple sources. RVWRMP has various combinations that it classifies as MUS. The schemes that combine micro-hydropower and irrigation are obvious multiple use schemes. Initially, in designing the gravity-flow piped supplies, the Kathmandu-based consultants were biased towards domestic uses only. Communities were not aware of options that they had not been offered in the past. Time for interaction with villagers for participatory designs was too limited. After some years, the project realized that virtually all gravity-flow drinking-water systems were used for multiple purposes anyway. The project started promoting homestead gardening, an innovation in this area, and started supporting these productive uses. This improved food security in this chronically food insecure region. The project also increasingly taps the potential benefits of multiple sources. For example, existing traditional spring sources for drinking water are maintained as back-up in case other sources fail. At the start, the project also established catchment committees parallel to local government, but this created confusion and they were abolished. Local government staff from different catchments easily find each other to address water resource and conservation issues that may arise across administrative boundaries.

Another lesson is that, certainly in the beginning, all parties were biased towards the quick, expensive new construction of larger schemes. The project staff wanted to show 'action' and the local contractors and wage labourers wanted employment.

A third lesson is that a legitimate, transparent and longer term area-wide master plan by local government serves at least two goals in addition to ensuring community-owned, needs-based plans. Other potential financers can also choose to finance prioritized actions, especially because the project tries to include them in the planning process from the outset. The Poverty Alleviation Fund (see Chapter 6) collaborates in this way. Further, transparent plans appeared effective in mitigating lobbying by the more powerful (Rautanen et al., 2014).

As RVWRMP's constellation follows statutory structures and procedures, lessons learnt can be replicated anywhere in Nepal, provided districts have access to both unconditional water grants or development grants (or opportunities to combine funding streams) and the necessary capacity as well as political support – which are all still major challenges. The importance of ensuring that funding is available to meet expressed needs, as did RVWRMP, appears to be vital. This becomes even clearer in the last MUS-by-design pilot project.

Strengthening community planning in local government: South Africa AWARD MUS pilot

The NGO AWARD in South Africa pioneered the planning phases of MUS-by-design in a third constellation: as support to communities to express their voices to local government according to the statutory Integrated Development Plan procedures. Supported by the Challenge Programme on Water and Food, AWARD facilitated a holistic diagnosis and prioritization process in 11 communities in Ward 16 of Bushbuckridge District Municipality. Resource mapping revealed a 'spaghetti' of overlaying earlier constructed and rehabilitated domestic and irrigation structures, many of which were defunct. The long list of identified needs included awareness-raising about vandalism, the promotion of homestead-based tanks, and the rehabilitation of infrastructure. The repair of a borehole came at the top of the list and was proposed for financing.

Unfortunately, the local government put that plan aside in favour of other pressing work that their superiors expected from them. Local government staff's fear that community initiatives might compete with their own municipal schemes may also have played a role. This experience shows the importance of a stronger link between planning processes and budgeting, a major challenge amid numerous parallel operating planning processes by local government and by line agencies and other stakeholders operating through local government, each with upward accountability (Maluleke et al., 2005; Dlamini and Cousins, 2009).

Conclusions and recommendations for scaling up MUS-by-design

This chapter described eight donor-supported projects that proved the concept of MUS-by-design for individuals and communities. Entry points are diverse: individual, affordable and multipurpose technologies; financing (through micro-credit arrangements); water as an integrated resource; or specific target groups (women). Some leveraged the WASH sub-sector, and others came from the irrigation sub-sector. More entry points, for example ecosystem services approaches, may open up in the future, each with its professional community that can be leveraged as a scaling-up partner.

In these MUS-by-design projects, the donors set the goal and allocate budgets for any water intervention that communities prioritize in decentralized and participatory planning and decision-making processes or by purchasing private technologies. Communities express their priorities to implementing agencies and local government, who are able to mobilize national and international funding and other resources to meet those needs (with the exception of the pilot in Bushbuckridge, South Africa). Thus, the long route to accountability becomes shorter while the short route is strengthened.

However, other well-known challenges of public services continue. The limited documentation available highlights spending pressure favouring elite capture and new construction (although other cases showed that communities opted for rehabilitation), and the continued single-use conventions of experts and line agencies in providing technical support.

Independent donor funding and implementation through independent agents in collaboration with local government allows pioneering and innovation. It also allows the involvement of the private sector, which the public sector may overlook. However, the replicating of lessons learnt may be limited to the own organization only. Also, with the exception of sustainable market supply chains of appropriate technologies, the sustainability of these projects once the donor leaves is a question.

The alternative is working more closely with, or entirely through, local government structures. This has the following disadvantages and advantages. On the negative side, this chapter highlighted that:

- Capacity of local government is weak; experienced and well-resourced agencies that support local government in the MUS pilot projects may be needed for many more years in the project zones, but also elsewhere where the model is replicated.
- Local governments may discourage support to self-supply; they may see this as competing with their own monopolistic water service provision and a means for clients to hold them more accountable.
- Local government may not be able to link the needs expressed in participatory assessments with funding to meet those needs; thus, local government remains deaf to people's needs.
- Local government faces many demands from political parties, national administrations, and various line agencies and others, each with upward accountability; local government's co-ordination of water-related responsibilities is a daunting task.

On the positive side, the MUS-by-design pilots showed that:

- Local government already provides important support to implementing agencies in information provision to projects and spreading project information to communities, selection of communities, providing staff to support participatory planning and implementation, systematic technical quality control and vetting of proposals, and in some cases access to post-construction support.

- Iterative, transparent planning through local government procedures builds capacity and mitigates capture by elites and politicians; it can attract funding from other governmental and non-governmental sources and thereby promote convergence and pooling of resources. Post-construction support can be integrated in such planning.
- As shown by RVWRMP Nepal, local government can be the sole implementer of MUS-by-design and lessons learnt can be scaled up nationwide, provided central funding and other support can be mobilized for any water intervention, and local planning and implementation capacity is available.

MUS-by-design is sector-based as it focuses on water and can be scaled up through partners in the water sector, and potentially broader natural resource management and ecosystems approaches. What happens and what can be learnt if programmes leave the choice for communities even more open, and also allow for other priorities, such as education, road, or health care in the new generation of local and community-driven development approaches?

CHAPTER 6

Implicit MUS in local and community-driven development

This chapter turns to water components in LCDD projects, as far as these water components have been documented. Especially in the case of MG-NREGS, research findings are presented that suggest that communities, their local authorities and local service provision officers do opt for MUS, at least to some extent. Other features of MG-NREGS include the scheme's own funding and nationwide implementation through local government. The chapter also presents examples of LCDD projects elsewhere, each with a different implementation constellation: through implementing agencies with own funding; through local government with own funding; and in support of local government planning without designated funding.

Keywords: LCDD, implicit MUS, MG-NREGS, local government, implementing agencies, India, Nepal, South Africa, Tanzania

Instead of channelling large amounts of financial and other resources from the top down to narrowly defined single-use or even multiple-use *water* projects, the new generation of local and community-driven development programmes is designed to channel many small amounts directly to communities for the projects of their choice. If communities opt for water, this project design implicitly provides the institutional space for communities to bring the five strengths of Chapter 3 to the table: their own assets, own priorities, for multiple benefits, from multipurpose infrastructure, while efficiently combining multiple sources. Does such 'implicit MUS' occur, and what can be learnt for scaling up MUS?

In trying to answer this question, the MUS Scoping Studies studied the evidence of water components in LCDD programmes. We present examples of the same constellations as in MUS-by-design: programmes implemented by donors and independent implementing agencies; programmes with own funding through local government (and in this case both state funding and donor funding); and capacity-building support to local government without own funding. These examples are listed in Table 6.1. The table also gives the total number of clients in these programmes, showing the generally large scale of projects, especially those through local government.

Unfortunately, the precise number of water projects and their clients and their proportion out of all project clients in these community-driven projects are unknown. The precise nature of water interventions is even less known. This is partly because of the same reasons mentioned earlier (innovation is recent and documentation and evaluation of public services is generally weak) and partly because the focus of the LCDD programmes is not specifically on water and even less on MUS. Single-use technical support in the identification of needs and design of projects might well have continued. The latter was found, for example, in the MUS Scoping Study for Ghana's Community-Based Rural Development Project and Social Opportunities Project. When communities opted for water projects, the (participatory) Community Water and Sanitation Agency was called in and applied its conventional single use domestic designs (Smits et al., 2011a). Administrative reporting requirements might also reflect conventional single-use administrations, or only main uses, and not all uses. Indeed, we assume that if MUS factually emerges, it is despite narrow specialism and silos, but because communities and local authorities mobilize support for MUS to tap its strengths.

Table 6.1 Employment generation and development grants of LCDD projects with water components

Public sector constellations	Employment generation (total no. of clients reached)	Development grants (total no. of clients reached)
Local government programmes (with state and/or donor funds)	India MG-NREGS (55 million labourers annually) South Africa: Community Work Programme (99,000 labourers since start)	Tanzania Social Action Fund (20,628,672 since start)
Donors with implementing agencies		Nepal Poverty Alleviation Fund (55,000 since start)
Support to local government planning		O&OD Tanzania (two-thirds of all rural local authorities)

The Mahatma Gandhi National Rural Employment Guarantee Scheme, the Poverty Alleviation Fund in Nepal, Tanzania's Social Action Fund, and Tanzania's Opportunities and Obstacles to Development (O&OD) tool mention a wide range of water projects. This allows some exploration of how the institutional space for MUS has been used and whether and how better technical support can further tap all strengths of MUS.

We first discuss the programme that is by far the largest and also relatively the best studied.

Mahatma Gandhi National Rural Employment Guarantee Scheme

India's Mahatma Gandhi National Rural Employment Guarantee Scheme reaches 55 million poor people per year, while creating small, demand-driven and locally appropriate projects. Pilot implementation of MG-NREGS started in 2005 and was rolled out nationwide by 2009. MG-NREGS aims to provide 100 days' paid labour per year to any rural citizen claiming the right to work as enshrined in the law. Employment guarantees for minimum wage automatically self-targets the poor. A minimum of 60 per cent of the total annual budget of US$9 billion reaches the poor in this way. Women constitute 48 per cent of the beneficiaries. In Kerala, where the state government implements MG-NREGS through Kudumbashree women's organization, this percentage is 90 per cent.

The other 40 per cent of the budget is for material and capacity-building investments to achieve the other goal of MG-NREGS: asset creation. The scheme devolves decision-making about the choice of works to community councils, with the technical support of officers at village, block, and district levels. The assets created allow for economic development so that wage workers do not need to work for minimum wages any more. Thus, the long-term exit strategy of MG-NREGS is poverty eradication.

In this decentralized, community-driven prioritization, two-thirds of the assets chosen are for water and drought proofing (Malik, 2011; Verma et al., 2012). Thus, MG-NREGS is the world's largest rural water project, investing about US$3 billion annually in water assets. Assets created include the digging and excavation of wells and ponds, pit-latrine digging, irrigation-canal rehabilitation, watershed management, groundwater recharge structures, forestry and plantations for soil conservation, land erosion prevention, river check dams, flood control, drainage in waterlogged areas, and gulley treatment. While most assets are communal, other investments are for individual assets of the marginalized Scheduled Castes and Tribes, such as pit latrines and irrigation, plantations, horticulture or other land development. In bottom-up water asset creation, there are no divides between water services for more uses and livelihoods and water conservation for the sustainable availability of resources, especially through groundwater recharge. These water works are labour intensive, which aligns well with the goal of employment creation. Data from a study of more than 140 best-performing MG-NREGS water assets in 75 villages across eight districts show that, on average, the labour and material investments in these assets can be recovered in a little over a year (Verma et al., 2011).

A comparison of these achievements with the strengths of MUS mentioned in Chapter 3 shows that the capitals of self-supply are leveraged and supported, for both communal and individual assets. Decentralized choice of assets and implementation strengthens and ensures local appropriateness of works and strengthens ownership, although the respective roles of local authorities and state officers, and intra-community hierarchies warrant more study. Well over half of the works generate multiple benefits from cost-effective multipurpose infrastructure (Malik, 2011; Verma et al., 2011). Efficient use of multiple conjunctive sources of local water cycles is central to groundwater recharge, check dams and watershed management, among other. Hence, MG-NREGS is implicitly, without any purposive design, also the world's largest MUS laboratory (Verma et al., 2011).

Accountability in fund allocation and spending is institutionalized in strict guidelines and procedures for transparent planning, prioritization, fund approval, implementation and evaluation – along the generic lines of LCDD and the MUS guidelines alike (Adank et al., 2012). With only a few additional dedicated MG-NREGS staff, local governments first enable all willing workers to obtain job cards. Within two months, action plans are discussed with communities and technically approved up to district level. Within the next month budgets are compiled and approved at district level. In the following two months, budgeted workplans are sent for approval to the state government and then to central government. In the next two months, communities and local government assess spillovers of preceding budgets and finalize current budgets. So within seven months, communities move from work identification to implementation. Attendance is registered and payments to personal or spouses' joint bank accounts and post offices follow within 14 days. All details of all these steps are entered into and monitored in open access electronic databases. Social audits are encouraged in which beneficiaries and NGOs can demand further accountability and expose corruption.

The match between top-down funding and the bottom-up 'pull' of local integrated needs and opportunities is not only facilitated by own funding for employment and own funding for broadly defined assets. MG-NREGS also promotes 'convergence' of the many parallel government programmes which each have their own narrow earmarked funding. By pooling financial resources, gaps are filled and overlaps avoided. In this way, the central managers formalize and promote creative integrated programme design and budgeting at district and lower levels. When water works go beyond the administrative boundaries, as in large-scale irrigation schemes or watershed programmes, the officers of the higher level blocks and districts concerned contact each other to collaborate.

Asset creation adds value to what the alternative of MG-NREGS would be (and some already perceive it as): a cash transfer programme. According to Verma and Shah (2012b) the goal of asset creation can be improved in eight ways:

- Pick the low-hanging fruit first, in particular by rehabilitating existing village water bodies and improving private lands (of the poor) with more reliable maintenance.
- Keep MG-NREGS demand-driven by avoiding a supply-driven administration under spending pressure which jeopardizes the quality of assets.
- Recognize the importance of assets by post-construction monitoring and capacity building of 'barefoot engineers'.
- Assign responsibility for maintenance, preferably before the works start, strengthening functioning local arrangements.
- Better equip MG-NREGS administration, especially in poor areas, to avoid the vicious circle of poorer performance, for example in payment schedules, and reducing demand.

- Build capacities of village institutions to become an effective demand system, for example by village leaders who can show their managerial skills through high-quality assets.
- Avoid alienating better-off farmers while maintaining MG-NREGS wage benefits, for example by general boosting of the agrarian economy.
- Get the performance measurement right and plan for an exit by improving economic conditions to reduce demand for minimum wage labour and monitoring the extensive database to that end.

Corruption does exist, however. A reason for Kerala's rule to allocate 90 per cent to labour costs and only 10 per cent to material costs is to avoid corruption in procurement. Indeed, corruption is increasingly exposed in India's media. While some point at the fact that this is petty corruption and at least spread among many more 'beneficiaries' than other forms of corruption, the extensive exposure is clearly affecting the scheme's reputation, which might even affect the form under which the scheme will continue if elections bring another government to power in the first leg of the long route to accountability.

Other LCDD programmes

Employment creation: Community Work Programme South Africa

The MG-NREGS approach was also a source of inspiration for South Africa to start its national Community Work Programme (CWP). This programme was piloted by NGOs starting in 2007 and has been rolled out through local government since 2010. It has reached 99,000 beneficiaries. The CWP reports also mention many diverse water-related activities: river cleaning; 45,000 home food gardens and 5,000 community clinics, crèches or school gardens; potable water and sanitation provision to homes, schools, clinics and communal buildings; maintenance activities such as the repair of leaks; cleaning irrigation canals; nutrient recycling through composting and waste management; water and land conservation and soil erosion prevention such as gulley treatment and managing grazing and watering of livestock; and bridge construction. As with MG-NREGS, these achievements reflect support to self-supply, local choice, multiple benefits from multipurpose infrastructure, and management of conjunctive water sources.

Development through implementing agencies: Poverty Alleviation Fund Nepal

Since 2004, the Poverty Alleviation Fund in Nepal has piloted the LCDD approach in support of the country's efforts to establish a new democratic state (PAF, 2010). The prime minister chairs the Board of Governors of the Poverty Alleviation Fund. The World Bank, International Development Association and IFAD contribute annually about US$35 million (2009/2010). Implementing partner organizations facilitate the establishment of community organizations and the identification, planning, fund disbursement, and implementation of sub-projects. Although the community action plan is incorporated into the planning process of the Village Development Committee and District Development Committee, funding streams are directly to partner organizations – partly because there are no elected local governments as yet. By 2011, the PAF had implemented 16,576 income-generation sub-projects, benefiting 550,000 people in 40 districts with low Human Development Indices.

Water projects figured to some extent. One of the four components is community infrastructure, which took about a quarter of the funds. It included water infrastructure for water supply and sanitation, small irrigation, river-bed land reclamation, water management, plastic tanks, sprinkler-drip systems, farmer-managed irrigation systems, and micro-hydro plants (PAF, 2010). The fund also implemented components of the WUMP in RVWRMP.

This diversity includes improvement of self-supply (farmer-managed irrigation) and choice, which may reflect local priorities. Ownership appeared important: the PAF project report compared the cost-effectiveness of these demand-driven participatory infrastructure projects although the type of infrastructure was not specified. A comparison was made between unit costs of selected infrastructure projects planned and executed by central government with their line agencies and with projects executed by community organizations. This showed that costs of community organization works are between 13 per cent and 47.5 per cent lower than central government costs. The report mentions factors such as the greater sense of ownership and more careful stewardship of resources which beneficiaries view as their own, and better knowledge of local prices and quality of local service providers than central agencies could reasonably possess (PAF, 2010). The schemes are administratively categorized as single use and single source; further research would be needed on the reasons for this. It may reflect continued influence of sub-sectoral mindsets.

Development through local government: Tanzania Social Action Fund

The Tanzania Social Action Fund (TASAF), which started in 2000, works through local government. Local government plays an important role in Tanzania as part of Nyerere's mission as expressed at a UN meeting in 1974: 'While other nations try to reach the moon, we are trying to reach the village'. Tanzania's current Decentralization by Devolution policy continues these efforts. In TASAF, donors such as the International Development Agency, DFID, and the World Food Programme established a national fund. Through ring-fenced financing, donors can still pursue specific aims, such as forestry development and environmental issues. Donors could promote MUS in this way too. By 2011, TASAF had reached 20,628,672 people. Between 2006 and mid-2011, a total of 12,237 sub-projects were received from local government authorities. Out of these, 10,526 sub-projects have been funded and valued at US$100 million. Besides rehabilitation of roads, the most frequent sub-projects of targeted infrastructure development are (in this order): construction of classrooms, improved water provision, construction or rehabilitation of health facilities, and other. 'Other' includes the construction of a few small irrigation schemes.

TASAF also has a specific public works component, which combines asset creation and wage employment creation for unskilled workers in labour-intensive projects. Communities choose the works. Many types of water sub-projects are reported: construction of *charco* dams for livestock watering and other uses, small irrigation schemes using both surface and groundwater, small earthen dams, rainwater harvesting techniques, shallow wells, watershed management, water tanks, drainage systems for storm water, restoration of degraded areas, gully treatment and erosion prevention, windmills, protection of water sources, rainwater harvesting, and market shed and associated facilities. This included both water development and conservation. As construction and earth works are labour intensive, employment creation goals may favour water interventions.

Almost half of the beneficiaries of the public works programme are women. Reportedly, women's participation in decision-making, signing cheques and leadership also increased to an average of 50 per cent. In some sub-projects women surpassed these benchmarks (TASAF, n.d.).

Strengthening community planning in local government: Tanzania Opportunities and Obstacles to Development tool

Tanzania developed and applies the Opportunities and Obstacles to Development tool (PMO-RALG, 2007, 2008) in support of local government. The Prime Minister's Office of Regional and Local Government is leading in this, in collaboration with the Japan International Cooperation Agency. The O&OD tool focuses on the decentralized first leg of the long route and on the short route to accountability between communities and local government authorities and service providers. Since 2001, more than two-thirds of the local government authorities in Tanzania have been trained. At national, district and ward level, facilitators are trained to support communities in expressing their voice and prioritizing their multi-sectoral needs. The identified priorities constitute multi-sectoral three-year community development plans that are updated annually.

As for AWARD's integrated water planning in South Africa, the O&OD planning supports local government staff and procedures, but is weakly linked to the budget planning and allocation processes of the second leg of the long route to accountability. As reported in evaluations (PMO-RALG, 2007, 2008; Taylor, 2011), district-level authorities receive the multi-sectoral community priority plans of their 60–100 villages. They have to sort the plans by hand and divide them into sectors with their funding streams. There is no one spreadsheet that provides an overview. All single-use water basket funds or education, health or agriculture sectors have their own top-down planning systems, which 'attach importance to effective and efficient implementation of interventions which meet the sectoral objectives and strategies'. For the sake of the top-down 'solid planning and budgeting system', district authorities are forced to prioritize those national plans over community plans. Local governments have started to receive a few untied funding streams. 'For fair and transparent funding', budget guidelines are to be used. However, these guidelines are delayed and keep changing. Even once the budgets are allocated, budgets still may change. Moreover, the community plans are too expensive for the available resources, while the O&OD process itself is also expensive. Thus, there is a mismatch between expressed needs and accountable disbursement of central funding.

Water supply pipes, irrigation schemes, streams and wetlands are all mentioned in the handbook for the situational analysis maps. However, without upfront funding to that end, even if an integrated community-driven MUS plan had been compiled, funding requirements would have forced officers to dissect it again according to the single-use sub-sectors entrenched in single-use basket funding.

Conclusions and recommendations for scaling up implicit MUS

Within the past decade, LCDD approaches have implicitly promoted demand-driven water interventions at very large scales. These approaches are highly appropriate for meeting the diverse basic and small-scale productive uses, and to fill the water sector's void in taking responsibility for public services to the poor that meet their productive needs as well. The programme constellations are similar to the MUS-by-design projects. LCDD through local government with own funding is the proven approach of MG-NREGS in which the decentralized long route to accountability and the short route to accountability are made to work together. Others are trying to replicate it. Treasuries and donors divide central funding to many small projects on the ground, according to clear and transparent guidelines for project development and conditions, intensive empowerment and capacity building, and transparent fund allocation, accountancy and social audits. The service is co-produced from the early planning phases onwards, with all sub-sectors relevant for water. National directives to promote convergence can further help to match bottom-up demands with public support.

LCDD projects by donors with implementing agencies depend on continued donor funding; this works better when various donors pool their resources into a central fund. The importance of guaranteed funding for outcomes of participatory planning becomes clear in the third constellation of programmes that support local government and rely on unconditional grants (which are limited for most local government) or on convergence and pooling of the funding from the many top-down parallel projects. This is difficult indeed; it warrants dissecting even integrated water proposals back into single-use interventions, if the proposals are not immediately buried under local government's other competing demands.

All projects reported a wide range of water development and conservation interventions, possibly reflecting the general success of LCDD for small infrastructure projects. Further research is recommended to reveal in much more detail whether and how communities and local authorities designed MUS. Questions include whether and how engineering, water-related health and wealth expertise, and expertise from other sectors was mobilized and aligned; whether and how the participatory planning process included all community members and facilitated the identification of priority actions; and whether and how the weaknesses of public services were addressed, with regard to problems such as supply-driven spending pressure, lack of sustainability (especially in infrastructure maintenance); and elite capture and corruption. Above all, such research will assess whether and how the five strengths of MUS are tapped and can be tapped better at the already large scales of LCDD projects.

CHAPTER 7
Conclusions and recommendations

After recapping the strengths of MUS, we conclude with the key lessons learnt at central level on the required but very gradual change in mandates of the specialist water sub-sectors' monitoring of construction targets, towards water services for a priority use and other uses, or for any uses that communities prioritize for broader human development outcomes. The key lessons learnt at local level revolve around the scaling up of participatory planning processes and co-production of services. The recommendation is to further consolidate the dialogue between public services reformers and the water sector in general, and MUS proponents in particular.

Keywords: human development performance, central re-alignment, local co-production of services

This book has explored the synergies between global public services reform and such reform in the water sector, in which MUS is the pivot. The accountability triangle of public services and related concepts allows an insightful analysis of experiences in piloting and scaling up MUS. We have shown how the WASH and irrigation sub-sectors have already adopted some measures to improve performance within their silos, and how MUS takes these trends forward across the sub-sectors and from the planning phase of services onwards. We conclude that the synergies revolve around the evidence and likelihood that placing people, with multiple water needs, at centre stage in water services contributes more effectively to gender-equitable poverty alleviation and human development than sub-sectoral approaches; and further, around the two main challenges for scaling up MUS: re-alignment of sectoral services at central levels and co-production of MUS at local levels.

The higher human development performance of MUS

We have shown that MUS entails five new proven or plausible strengths to improve human development outcomes of water services.

1. MUS leverages and supports self-supply. Tapping communities' human, financial, technical, physical, and institutional capital is more cost-effective and gives communities choice and power vis-à-vis public service providers.

2. MUS meets people's priorities, which ensures more ownership and local appropriateness of choices, especially for diverse productive water uses. This improves sustainability.
3. MUS promotes multiple uses, leading to broader mutually reinforcing livelihood benefits and human development outcomes.
4. MUS designs multipurpose infrastructure as the rule, which is more cost-effective. The incremental costs needed to expand single-use infrastructure to multiple-use infrastructure lead to very high benefits. Moreover, by planning for these uses, damage of unplanned uses is avoided.
5. MUS efficiently uses and re-uses water from multiple water sources in the local water cycle, which offers more options and resilience.

Human development outcomes and re-alignment at central levels

At central levels, the main challenge in realizing MUS at scale is the re-alignment of the sub-sectors. We have analysed how funding, engineering expertise, and expertise to render water uses more beneficial through accompanying measures (the expertise to create health and wealth) are tightly locked in silos. The sub-sectors are dominated by the expertise to create health or wealth and the ultimate human development outcomes of that single use. This consolidates the assumption that water can only be used for that purpose, even if communities have other priorities as well – as they typically have.

The book has analysed how the domestic-plus and irrigation-plus approaches suggest that central policymakers and senior managers, who promote an outcome-based services approach of providing water in agreed quantities, of agreed quality at agreed times and sites, can well promote their priority water use *and* other water uses for broader human development outcomes.

The challenge is to unlock the expertise to create health and wealth from the top-down hierarchical silos, so a question for further consideration is how this expertise can be provided in a demand-driven manner, and more effectively.

With regard to engineering expertise and other public support to operate and maintain infrastructure, the question is how infrastructure planning and design can become more participatory to meet communities' priority uses. Communities, in particular the poor and women, need to have more choice in individual or communal infrastructure, operation and maintenance obligations, and in the site of the infrastructure. Private technology suppliers can play a strong role, while governments and NGOs can assist in rendering technologies more affordable. More work is also needed on further subsidization and financing facilities to ensure that public and private support reaches poor men and especially poor women.

In addition to reshaping such indispensable expertise, central-level water policymakers and senior managers need to decentralize decision-making about investments to communities and their authorities – another field where public service providers can learn from each other. Nevertheless, water professionals have unique competencies and responsibilities in ensuring that public funding for water services contributes to achieving the international and national policy commitments to gender-equitable poverty alleviation. In order to take up this responsibility, we identified the need to start a conversation on a new common vision on priorities in which the water sub-sectors collaborate and learn from each other instead of defending narrow contradictory sub-sector views.

Such vision could prioritize, first, accelerating efforts for universal water supplies for basic domestic uses, out of which at least 3–5 lpcd should be safe, both for women's empowerment and for health. A second priority would be to meet basic productive water uses, beyond the few pockets of public irrigation schemes, for which neither the WASH nor the irrigation sub-sector has taken responsibility in the past. Domestic-plus, which tends to favour women and also reaches the landless and disabled, is a practical way to achieve that goal. Third, statutory water law reform is urgently warranted to respect and protect poor people's basic domestic *and* small-scale productive water uses.

Scaling up MUS requires public funding to reach its goal, together with both forms of demand-driven expertise, and decentralization of decision-making about fund allocation to many small projects co-produced by communities and their authorities. Funding can be leveraged from the WASH and irrigation sub-sectors that maintain their priority use (in the +plus approaches), or from any funding source, but usually from within the water sector, that sets as its goal general water intervention according to people's priorities (MUS-by-design). Considerable funding also appears to come from donor- and state-funded LCDD programmes that leave the choice of the intervention to communities. If communities opt for water interventions, they have institutional space to apply MUS (implicit MUS).

Co-production of services at local levels

The third field of synergies between public services reform and MUS concerns the co-production of services at local levels. While the +plus approaches give more discretionary power to their local service provision officers, decentralization and co-production goes further: processes of participatory planning are facilitated and funding is mobilized for the results of these processes. Private sector support, for example, for affordable technology supply chains complements this.

Implementing agencies with own funding have more autonomy to innovate and to proof the concept of MUS-by-design, as also known for agencies implementing LCDD pilot projects. MUS-by-design and LCDD projects with own state or donor funding are also implemented through local government, also at very large scales. MUS-by-design fits and strengthens iterative local government planning and implementation procedures, including co-ordination with other sectors, such as transport, market or energy.

However, without guaranteed funding for the priorities identified in the participatory planning process, the expressed needs risk falling on local government's deaf ears because of their lack of unconditional monies and because other top-down demands with pre-defined central goals compete for their attention.

Communities identified a broad range of water interventions, which reflected a high local diversity in priorities. This encompassed multiple water sources in the water cycle and many productive uses that have no clear institutional home as yet in government structures.

Persistent challenges of public services were also reported, where exchange and joint learning on possible solutions will also be rewarding. One example is male elite capture, which was partially mitigated by transparent planning and avoidance of spending pressure. Women's exclusion can be mitigated by a widely pursued priority for domestic uses across the water sector. More work is especially needed on smart subsidies for the poor. Another persistent challenge is the risk of weak cost recovery and low infrastructure sustainability.

Recommendations

The strong links between global reform in public services and MUS in the water sector warrant consolidated dialogue to realize the five strengths of MUS for a more pro-poor and gender-equitable water services. The available knowledge points at the 'why' of such dialogue and also the broad directions on 'how to' realize such better performance. More rigorous and comparative documentation, analysis and ex-post evaluation of all projects described and other existing literature will already greatly deepen knowledge. Implicit MUS should be made explicit. The design and implementation of future piloting and especially scaling up can generate further insights of well-analysed action-research.

In this dialogue, water specialists can deepen expertise on the five strengths of MUS, including expertise of the specificities of water resources development and management, participatory engineering design expertise, and expertise to render water more beneficial for multifaceted livelihoods.

The public sector reform will continue generating multi-sectoral LCDD projects that provide the implicit space for MUS, also in co-production with the many other sectors relevant for water. Insights from public sector reform will inform the co-production of MUS-by-design programmes from central to local levels and vice versa, and their further scaling up. Solutions for spending pressure, male elite capture, cost recovery and post-construction support, and other typical flaws in the public sector will also be addressed more productively in more dialogue.

Lastly, communities' self-supply and their priorities, which are the basis for MUS, need to be better understood. After all, the five strengths of MUS only mirror how communities, who are not constrained by sectoral mindsets, have developed and managed water resources since time immemorial.

References

Adank, M.D. 2006. *Linking Multiple Use Services and Self Supply Principles*. Paper prepared for 5th Rural Water Supply Network Forum, 27–30 November, Accra, Ghana.

Adank, M., Jeths, M., Belete, B., Chaka, S. Lema, Z., Tamiru, D. and Abebe, Z. 2008. 'The costs and benefits of multiple uses of water: the case of Gorogutu Woreda of East Hararghe Zone, Oromiya Regional States, Eastern Ethiopia', *RiPPLE Working Paper 4*. <www.rippleethiopia.org/documents/ stream/20081006-wp7-mus-study> [accessed 16 August 2013].

Adank, M., Kumasi, T., Abbey, E., Dickinson, N., Dzansi, P., Atengdem, J., Laari Chimbar, T. and Effah, E. 2013. *The Status of Rural Water Supply Services in Ghana: A Synthesis of Findings from 3 Districts. Triple-S Working Paper*. Accra, Ghana: CWSA (Community Water and Sanitation Agency)/IRC International Water and Sanitation Centre. <www.waterservicesthatlast. org/media/publications/the_status_of_rural_water_supply_services_in_ ghana> [accessed 3 February 2014].

Adank, M., van Koppen, B. and Smits, S. 2012. *Guidelines for Planning and Providing Multiple-use Water Services*. MUS Group publication. The Hague: IRC International Water and Sanitation Centre; Pretoria: International Water Management Institute.

Alberts, J.H. and van der Zee, J.J. 2003. *A Multi-sectoral Approach to Sustainable Rural Water Supply: The Role of the Rope Handpump in Nicaragua*. Proceedings of International Symposium on Water Poverty and Productive Uses at the Household Level, Muldersdrift, South Africa. <www.irc.nl/page/8052> [accessed 3 February 2014].

Alberts, J.H. and van der Zee, J.J. 2004. 'A multi-sectoral approach to sustainable rural water supply: the role of the rope handpump in Nicaragua', in P. Moriarty, J. Butterworth and B. van Koppen (eds), *Beyond Domestic: Case Studies on Poverty and Productive Uses of Water at the Household Level*. The Hague: IRC, NRI, IWMI. <www.irc.nl/page/6129> [accessed 3 February 2014].

AME Study Group on Functional Organization. 1988. 'Organizational renewal – tearing down the functional silos', *AME Target* (Summer): 4–16. <www.ame.org/sites/default/files/target_articles/88q2a1.pdf> [accessed 3 February 2014]

Bahri, A., Sally, H., Namara, R.E., McCartney, M., Awulachew, S.B., van Koppen, B. and van Rooijen, D. 2010. *Integrated Watershed Management: Towards Sustainable Solutions in Africa*. Presented at 6th Biennial Rosenberg International Forum on Water Policy, 23–27 June, Zaragoza, Spain. <www.zaragoza.es/contenidos/medioambiente/cajaAzul/BahriACC.pdf> [accessed 3 February 2014].

Bakker, M., Barker, R., Meinzen-Dick, R. and Konradsen, F. (eds). 1999. 'Multiple uses of water in irrigated areas: a case study from Sri Lanka', *SWIM Paper No.8*. Colombo: International Water Management Institute.

Bangladesh Bureau of Statistics. 2000. *Statistical Yearbook of Bangladesh*. Dhaka: Bangladesh Bureau of Statistics.

Basnet, G. and van Koppen, B. 2011. *Multiple Use Water Services Scoping Study in Nepal*. Kathmandu: International Water Management Institute, IRC International Water and Sanitation Center and The Rockefeller Foundation. <www.musgroup.net> [accessed 16 August 2013].

Bey, V., Abisa, J. and Magara, P. 2014. *Assessment of the Performance of the Service Delivery Model for Point Sources in Uganda: Final Research Report*. Kampala, Uganda: Triple-S.

Binswanger, Hans P. and Nguyen, T.-V. 2005. 'A step-by-step guide to scale up community-driven development', in B. van Koppen, J.A. Butterworth and I.J. Juma (eds), *African Water Laws: Plural Legislative Frameworks for Rural Water Management in Africa*, Proceedings of a workshop held in Johannesburg, South Africa, 26–28 January. Pretoria: International Water Management Institute. <http://projects.nri.org/waterlaw/AWLworkshop/papers.htm#BINSWANGER> [accessed 3 February 2014].

Binswanger-Mkhize, H.P., de Regt, J.P. and Spector, S. (eds). 2009. *Scaling Up Local & Community Driven Development (LCDD). A Real World Guide to its Theory and Practice*. Amsterdam: Royal Tropical Institute. <http://www.kit.nl/kit/Publication?item=2769> [accessed 3 February 2014].

Boelee, E., Laamrani, H. and van der Hoek, W. 2007. 'Multiple use of irrigation water for improved health in dry regions of Africa and South-Asia', *Irrigation and Drainage* 56: 43–51. <http://dx.doi.org/10.1002/ird.287>.

Boelens, R., Bustamante, R. and de Vos, H. 2007. 'Legal pluralism and the politics of inclusion, recognition and contestation of local water rights in the Andes', in Barbara van Koppen, Mark Giordano and John Butterworth (eds), *Community-based Water Law and Water Resource Management Reform in Developing Countries. Comprehensive Assessment of Water Management in Agriculture Series 5*, pp. 96–113. Wallingford, UK: CABI Publishers.

Boelens, R., Dávila, G. and Menchu, R. (eds). 1998. *Searching for Equity: Conceptions of Justice and Equity in Peasant Irrigation*. Assen, The Netherlands: Van Gorcum.

Bolding, A., Post Uiterweer, N.C. and Schippers, J. 2010. 'The fluid nature of hydraulic property: a case study of Mukudu, Maira and Penha Longa irrigation furrows in the upper Revue River, Manica District, Mozambique', in P. van der Zaag (ed.), *What Role of Law in Promoting and Protecting the Productive Uses of Water by Smallholder Farmers?* [unpublished project report] pp. 105–36. Delft: UNESCO-IHE.

Butterworth, J. 2012. *Ten Key Steps in the Community Managed Project (CMP) Approach to Rural Water Supply. CMP approach: Effective and Sustainable WASH Services*. COWASH. <http://www.rural-water-supply.net/en/resources/details/357> [accessed 16 August 2013].

Butterworth, J., Sutton, S. and Mekonta, L. 2013. 'Self-supply as a complementary water services delivery model in Ethiopia', *Water Alternatives* 6(3): 405–23. <www.irc.nl/docsearch/title/182399> [accessed 3 February 2014].

Butterworth, J., Visscher, J.T. and van Steenbergen, F. with contributions from E. Boelee, M. Adank, Z. Abebe and B. van Koppen. 2011. *Multiple Use Water Services Scoping Study in Ethiopia*. Addis Ababa: International Water Management Institute, IRC International Water and Sanitation Center and The Rockefeller Foundation. <www.musgroup.net> [accessed 16 August 2013].

Chambers, R. 2010. 'Paradigms, poverty and adaptive pluralism', *IDS Working Paper 344*. Brighton, UK: Institute of Development Studies.

Community Managed Projects Ethiopia (CMPE) (no date) <www.cmpethiopia. org> [accessed 3 February 2014].

Coward, E.W., Jr. 2006. 'Property landscapes in motion'. Keynote address, International Association for the Study of Common Property 11th Biennial Global Conference, Bali, Indonesia, June. <www.iasc-commons. org/sites/all/IASC_Conferences/2006/Coward_Walt_Bali_Keynote.pdf> [accessed 16 August 2013].

Cullis, J. and van Koppen, B. 2007. 'Applying the Gini Coefficient to measure inequality of water use in the Olifants River Water Management Area', *IWMI Research Report 113*. Colombo: International Water Management Institute.

Cullis, J. and van Koppen, B. 2008. 'Applying the Gini coefficient to measure the distribution of water use and benefits of water use in South Africa's provinces'. Paper presented at the Water for Growth and Development Session, 17 August, Stockholm Water Week, Stockholm, Sweden: Stockholm International Water Institute. <http://hdl.handle.net/10568/21324> [accessed 3 February 2014].

de Kemp, A., Faust, J. and Leiderer, S. 2011. *Between High Expectations and Reality: An Evaluation of Budget Support in Zambia (2005–2010). Synthesis Report*. The Hague: IOB (Policy and Operations Evaluation Department, Netherlands Ministry of Foreign Affairs).

de Lange, M. and Penning de Vries, F.W.T. 2003. 'Integrated approaches to natural resource management: theory and practice', in D. Beukes, M. Villiers, S. Mkhize, H. Sally, L. van Rensburg (eds), *Farming Systems Conducive to Soil Water Conservation*, pp. 172–80, Proceedings of the Symposium and Workshop on Water Conservation Technologies for Sustainable Dryland Agriculture in Sub-Saharan Africa (WCT). Pretoria: ARC-Institute for Soil, Climate and Water.

de Regt, J.P. 2005. 'Water in rural communities', in B. van Koppen, J.A. Butterworth, and I. Juma (eds), *African Water Laws: Plural Legislative Frameworks for Rural Water Management in Africa*. Proceedings of a workshop held in Johannesburg, South Africa, 26–28 January. Pretoria: International Water Management Institute.

Department for International Development (DFID). 2013. *Water, Sanitation and Hygiene: Evidence Paper*. London: DFID. <https://www.gov.uk/government/publications/water-sanitation-and-hygiene-evidence-paper> [accessed 3 February 2014].

Dlamini, V.G. and Cousins, T. 2009. 'Case study on Bushbuckridge water service delivery challenges in the context of integrated water resource management (IWRM) and sustainable water and sanitation services (WATSAN): turning advocacy into action in the South African water sector'. Bushbuckridge, South Africa: Association for Water and Rural Development (AWARD).

Department of Water Affairs, South Africa (DWA). 2013. *Africa's Second National Water Resource Strategy 2*. Pretoria: DWA. <www.dwaf.gov.za/nwrs/NWRS2013.aspx> [accessed 3 February 2014].

Ensor, P.S. 1988. 'The functional silo syndrome', *AME Target*: 16. <www.ame.org/sites/default/files/documents/88q1a3.pdf> [accessed 3 February 2014].

Food and Agriculture Organization (FAO). 2010. *Mapping Systems and Services for Multiple Uses in Fenhe Irrigation District, Kirindi Oya Irrigation Settlement, Bac Hung Hai Irrigation and Drainage Scheme. Shahapur Branch Canal*. Rome: FAO.

FAO. 2013. 'AQUASTAT: FAO's information systems on water and agriculture'. <www.fao.org/nr/water/aquastat/main/index.stm> [accessed 12 December 2013].

Fonseca, C., Smits, S., Nyarko, K., Naafs, A. and Franceys, R. 2013. 'Financing capital maintenance of rural water supply systems: Current practices and future options', *WASHCost Working Paper 9*. The Hague: IRC International Water and Sanitation Centre.

Foster, V. and Briceño-Garmendia, C. (eds). 2010. *Africa's Infrastructure. A Time for Transformation*. Washington, DC: Agence Francaise de Développement and World Bank <http://dx.doi.org/10.1596/978-0-8213-8041-3>.

Funder, M., Bustamante, R., Cossio, V., Huong, P.T.M., van Koppen, Barbara, Mweemba, C., Nyambe, I., Phuong, L.T.T. and Skielboe, T. 2012. 'Strategies of the poorest in local water conflict and cooperation: evidence from Vietnam, Bolivia and Zambia', *Water Alternatives*, 5(1): 20–36 <www.water-alternatives.org/> [accessed 3 February 2014].

González de Asís, M., O'Leary, D., Ljung, P. and Butterworth, J. 2009. *Improving Transparency, Integrity and Accountability in Water Supply and Sanitation: Action, Learning, Experiences*. Washington, DC: The World Bank Institute and Transparency International. <http://dx.doi.org/10.1596/978-0-8213-7892-2>.

Government of India (GoI). 2011. *Faster, Sustainable and More Inclusive Growth: An Approach to the Twelfth Five Year Plan*. New Delhi: Planning Commission, GoI. <http://planningcommission.nic.in/plans/planrel/12appdrft/approach_12plan.pdf> [accessed 3 February 2014].

Hall, R.P. 2012. 'The productive use of rural domestic water in Senegal and Kenya and Its relationship to system sustainability'. Presented at Stockholm World Water Week, 30 August, Stockholm, Sweden.

Hall, R.P., van Koppen, B. and van Houweling, E. 2013. 'The human right to water: the importance of domestic and productive water rights', *Science and Engineering Ethics*, December <http://dx.doi.org/10.1007/s11948-013-9499-3>.

Harvey, P.A. and Reed, R.A. 2006. 'Community-managed water supplies in Africa: sustainable or dispensable?', *Community Development Journal* 42(3): 365–78. <http://dx.doi.org/10.1093/cdj/bsl001>.

Hussain, I., Wijerathna, D., Arif, S.S., Murtiningrum, Mawarni, A. and Suparmi. 2006. 'Irrigation, productivity and poverty linkages in irrigation systems in Java, Indonesia', *Water Resources Management* 20(3): 313–36 <http://dx.doi.org/10.1007/s11269-006-0079-z>.

Hutton, G. and Haller, L. 2004. *Evaluation of the Costs and Benefits of Water and Sanitation Improvements at the Global Level*. Geneva: World Health Organization. <www.who.int/water_sanitation_health/wsh0404/en/> [accessed 3 February 2014].

Hutton, G., Haller, L. and Bartram, J. 2007. *Economic and Health Effects of Increasing Coverage of Low Cost Household Drinking-Water Supply and Sanitation Interventions to Countries Off-track to Meet MDG Target 10*. Geneva: World Health Organization. <www.who.int/water_sanitation_health/economic/mdg10_offtrack/en/> [accessed 3 February 2014].

Improve International. 2012. *Statistics on Water & Sanitation System Failures* [online] <http://improveinternational.wordpress.com/handy-resources/sad-stats/> [accessed September 2013].

Joint Monitoring Programme (JMP). 2012. *Proposal for Consolidated Drinking Water, Sanitation and Hygiene Targets, Indicators and Definitions*. Geneva: JMP <www.worldwewant2015.org/node/304917> [accessed 3 February 2014].

Komakech, C.H. 2013. *Emergence and Evolution of Endogenous Water Institutions in an African River Basin: Local Water Governance and State Intervention in the Pangani River Basin, Tanzania*, PhD thesis. Delft: UNESCO-IHE and International Water Management Institute.

Komakech, C.H. and van der Zaag, P. 2011. 'Understanding the emergence and functioning of river committees in a catchment of the Pangani basin, Tanzania', *Water Alternatives*, 4(2): 197–222 <www.water-alternatives.org/index.php?option=com_content&task=view&id=157&Itemid=1> [accessed 3 February 2014].

Komakech, C.H., van der Zaag, P. and van Koppen, B. 2012a. 'The last will be first: conflict over water transfers from subsistence irrigation to cities in the Pangani river basin, Tanzania', *Water Alternatives*, 5(3): 700–20 <www.water-alternatives.org/index.php?option=com_content&task=view&id=223&Itemid=1> [accessed 3 February 2014].

Komakech, C.H., van der Zaag, P. and van Koppen, B. 2012b. 'Dynamics between water asymmetry, inequality and heterogeneity sustain canal institutions in Makanya catchment, Tanzania', *Water Policy*, 14(5): 800–20 <http://dx.doi.org/10.2166/wp.2012.196>.

Lankford, B.A. 2013. *Resource Efficiency Complexity and the Commons: The Paracommons and Paradoxes of Natural Resource Losses, Wastes and Wastages.* Abingdon, UK: Earthscan Publications.

Lankford, B.A., Merrey, D.J., Cour, J. and Hepworth, N. 2007. 'From integrated to expedient: An adaptive framework for river basin management in developing countries', *IWMI Research Report 110.* Colombo, Sri Lanka: International Water Management Institute.

Lockwood, H. and Smits, S. 2011. *Supporting Rural Water Supply: Moving Towards a Service Delivery Approach.* Rugby, UK: Practical Action Publishing <http://dx.doi.org/10.3362/9781780440699>.

Malano, H. and van Hofwegen, P. 1999. 'Management of irrigation and drainage systems: a service approach', *IHE Monograph Series.* Rotterdam: Balkema Publishing.

Malik, R.P.S. 2011. 'Rural water security through livelihood program', unpublished. New Delhi: International Water Management Institute.

Maluleke, T., Thomas, V., Cousins, T., Smits, S. and Moriarty, P. 2005. 'Securing water to enhance local livelihoods (SWELL): community-based planning of multiple uses of water in partnership with service providers. Introduction to the methodology'. South Africa: AWARD. <www.musgroup.net/home/meetings_and_events/the_cpwf_mus_project/basins_countries/limpopo_basin_cpwf_mus_studies/limpopo_basin_outputs/south_africa_introduction_to_swell_securing_water_to_enhance_local_livelihoods_methodology> [accessed 15 August 2013].

Marks, S.J. and Davis, J. 2012. 'Does user participation lead to sense of ownership for rural water systems? Evidence from Kenya', *World Development* 40(8): 1569–76 <http://dx.doi.org/10.1016/j.worlddev.2012.03.011>.

Mehari, A., van Steenbergen, F. and Schultz, B. 2007. 'Water rights and rules, and management in spate irrigation systems in Eritrea, Yemen and Pakistan', in Barbara van Koppen, Mark Giordano and John Butterworth (eds), *Community-based Water Law and Water Resource Management Reform in Developing Countries. Comprehensive Assessment of Water Management in Agriculture Series 5.* Wallingford, UK: CABI Publishers.

Mehta, L., Leach, M., Newell, P., Scoones, I., Sivaramakrishnan, K. and Way, S. 2001. 'Exploring understandings of institutions and uncertainty: new directions in natural resource management'. *IDS Discussion Paper No. 372.* Brighton, UK: Institute for Development Studies. <www.eldis.org/vfile/upload/1/document/0708/DOC7794.pdf> [accessed 3 February 2014].

Mehta, L., Veldwisch, G.J. and Franco, J. 2012. 'Introduction to the Special Issue: Water grabbing? Focus on the (re)appropriation of finite water resources', *Water Alternatives* 5(2): 193–207. <www.water-alternatives.org/index.php?option=com_content&task=view&id=45&Itemid=1> [accessed 3 February 2014].

Meinzen-Dick, R. 1997. 'Valuing the multiple uses of water', in M. Kay, T. Franks, L. Smith (eds), *Water: Economics, Management and Demand,* pp. 50–8. London: E&FN Spon.

Meinzen-Dick, R. and Zwarteveen, M. 1998. 'Gendered participation in water management: Issues and illustrations from water users' associations in South Asia', in D. Merrey and S. Baviskar (eds), *Gender Analysis and Reform of Irrigation Management: Concepts, Cases and Gaps in Knowledge. Proceedings of the Workshop on Gender and Water, September 1997*. Colombo, Sri Lanka: International Water Management Institute.

Merrey, D., 1996. *Institutional Design Principles for Accountability in Large Irrigation Systems. Research Report 8*. Colombo, Sri Lanka: International Water Management Institute.

MG-NREGS (no date) <www.nrega.nic.in> [website].

Mikhail, M. and Yoder, R. 2008. *Multiple Use Water Service Implementation in Nepal and India: Experience and Lessons forSscale-up*. Lakewood, Colorado: International Development Enterprises, Challenge Program on Water and Food, and International Water Management Institute. <www.ideorg.org/OurStory/IDE_multi_use_water_svcs_in_nepal_india_8mb.pdf> [accessed 3 February 2014].

Millennium Ecosystem Assessment. 2005. *Ecosystems and Human Wellbeing. Synthesis*. Washington, DC: Island Press. <www.millenniumassessment.org/documents/document.356.aspx.pdf> [accessed 15 August 2013].

Molden, D. 2007. *Water for Life: A Comprehensive Assessment of Water Management in Agriculture*. London: Earthscan, and Colombo: International Water Management Institute. <www.iwmi.cgiar.org/assessment/Publications/books.htm> [accessed 3 February 2014].

Molden, D., Burton, M. and Bos, M.G. 2007. 'Performance assessment, irrigation service delivery and poverty reduction: Benefits of improved system management', *Irrigation and Drainage* 56: 307–32 <http://dx.doi.org/10.1002/ird.313>.

Molle, F. and Renwick, M. 2005. 'Economics and politics and of water resources development: Uda Walawe Irrigation Project, Sri Lanka', *Research Report 87*. Colombo, Sri Lanka: International Water Management Institute. <www.iwmi.cgiar.org/Publications/IWMI_Research_Reports/PDF/pub087/Report87.pdf> [accessed 3 February 2014].

Moriarty, P., Butterworth, J. and van Koppen, B. (eds). 2004. 'Beyond domestic: case studies on poverty and productive uses of water at the household level', *IRC Technical Papers Series 41*. Delft: IRC, NRI, and IWMI. <www.irc.nl/page/6129> [accessed 3 February 2014].

Moriarty, P., Smits, S.; Butterworth, J. and Franceys, R. 2013. 'Trends in rural water supply: towards a service delivery approach', *Water Alternatives* 6 (3): 329–49. <www.irc.nl/page/81408> [accessed 3 February 2014].

Mukherji, A., Facon, T., Molden, D. and Chartres, C. 2010. 'Growing more food with less water: how can revitalizing Asia's irrigation help?', Paper for Water: Crisis and Choices – An ADB and Partners Conference, October. IWMI and FAO. <http://dx.doi.org/10.2166/wp.2011.146>.

MUS Group. 2013. *Publications database* [online] <www.musgroup.net/ ccm_eztag_find/main/search/34?q=&t[78][]=104&t[78][]=103&t[80] []=111&t[77][]=98&dn=1653&s=1> [accessed 11 December 2013].

Naidoo, N., Maine, G., Vrdoljak, M. and Chidley, C. 2009. 'Productive use of domestic piped water for sustaining livelihoods in poor households. Water Research Commission Report Project K5/1666 TT 412/09'. Pretoria: Water Research Commission and Nemai Consulting. <www.wrc.org. za/Pages/DisplayItem.aspx?ItemID=8605&FromURL=%2fPages%2fKH_ DocumentsList.aspx%3fdt%3d1%26su%3dc4%26ms%3d4%253b11%2 53b> [accessed 15 August 2013].

National Sample Survey Organisation (NSSO). 2005. 'Situation assessment survey of farmers: some aspects of farming. 59th Round, January – December 2003. Report 496 (59/33/3).' New Delhi: Department of Statistics, Government of India.

Nguyen-Khoa, S., Smith, L. and Lorenzen, K. 2005. 'Impacts of irrigation on inland fisheries: appraisals in Laos and Sri Lanka', *Comprehensive Assessment Research Report 7*. Colombo, Sri Lanka: Comprehensive Assessment Secretariat. <www.iwmi.cgiar.org/assessment/files_new/ publications/CA%20Research%20Reports/CA-RR7_final.pdf> [accessed 3 February 2014].

Nielsen, R., Hanstad, T. and Rolfes, L. 2006. 'Implementing homestead plot programmes: experience from India', *Working Paper 23 Livelihood Support Programme Access to Natural Resources Sub-Programme*. Rome: FAO and Rural Development Institute. <www.fao.org/sd/dim_pe4/pe4_061102_en.htm> [accessed 3 February 2014].

Noel, S., Hoang, T.P., Soussan, J. and Lovett, J. 2010. 'The impact of domestic water on household enterprises: evidence from Vietnam', *Water Policy* 12(2): 237–47. <www.sei-international.org/publications?pid=1720> [accessed 3 February 2014].

Organisation for Economic Co-operation and Development (OECD). 2008. *Paris Declaration on Aid Effectiveness and Accra Agenda for Action*. Paris: OECD.

Onda, K., LoBuglio, J. and Bartram, J. 2012. 'Global access to safe water: accounting for water quality and the resulting impact on MDG progress', *International Journal Of Environmental Research and Public Health* 9: 880–94 <http://dx.doi.org/10.3390/ijerph9030880>.

Poverty Alleviation Fund (PAF). 2010. *Annual Progress Report (2009/2010)*. Kathmandu: PAF. <www.pafnepal.org.np/uploads/document/file/Annual-Report-2009-2010.pdf> [accessed 3 February 2014].

Palanisami, K. and Meinzen-Dick, R. 2001. 'Tank performance and multiple uses in Tamil Nadu, South India', *Irrigation & Drainage Systems* 15(2): 173–95.

Palanisami, K., Meinzen-Dick, R., Giordano, M., van Koppen, B., and Ranganathan, C.R. 2011 'Tank performance and multiple uses in Tamil Nadu, South India: comparison of two time periods (1996–97 and

2009–10)', *Irrigation and Drainage Systems*, 25(1): 121–34 <http://dx.doi.org/10.1007/s10795-011-9114-1>.

Paul, S. 1994. 'Does voice matter? For public accountability, yes', *Policy Research Working Paper Series No.1388*. Washington, DC: World Bank.

Pavelic, P., Villholth, K.G. and Verma, S. 2013. 'Identifying the barriers and pathways forward for expanding the use of groundwater for irrigation in Sub-Saharan Africa', *Water International*, Special Issue Sustainable Groundwater Development for Improved Livelihoods in Sub-Saharan Africa, Part 1, 38(4): 363–8 <http://dx.doi.org/10.1080/02508060.2013.821643>.

Penning de Vries, F. and Ruaysoongnern, S. 2010. 'Multiple sources of water for multiple purposes in Northeast Thailand', *IWMI Working Paper 137*. Colombo, Sri Lanka:International Water Management Institute. <www.iwmi.cgiar.org/Publications/Working_Papers/working/WOR137.pdf> [accessed 3 February 2014].

Pérez de Mendiguren Castresana, J.C. 2004. 'Productive uses of water at the household level: evidence from Bushbuckridge, South Africa', in P. Moriarty, J. Butterworth and B. van Koppen (eds), *Beyond domestic: Case studies on poverty and productive uses of water at the household level. IRC Technical Papers Series 41*. Delft: the Netherlands. <www.irc.nl/page/8055> [accessed 3 February 2014].

Pezon, C. 1999. 'La gestion du service d'eau potable en France de 1850 à 1995', *Thèse ES Sciences de Gestion*. Paris: Presses du CEREM, Conservatoire National des Arts et Métiers.

Pezon, C., Agognon, F. and Bassono, R. 2013. 'Coût, performance et régulation des petits réseaux ; Étude de six AEPS dans la région du Sahel', *Document de recherche No.2*. The Hague, the Netherlands: IRC International Water and Sanitation Centre.

Prime Minister's Office Regional Administration and Local Government (PMO–RALG). 2007. *The Opportunities and Obstacles to Development: A Community Participatory Planning Methodology*. Dodoma, Tanzania: PMO–RALG.

PMO–RALG. 2008. *The Study on Improvements of O&OD Planning Process*. Dodoma, Tanzania: PMO–RALG.

Ramaru, J. and Hagmann, J. 2012. *Workshop Documentation MUS Roundtable Workshop* [pdf]. Bellagio Conference Center, Italy, 3–7 September. <www.musgroup.net/content/download/1363/11917/file/MUS%20Bellagio%20Documentation.pdf.> [accessed 15 August 2013].

Rautanen, S-L., van Koppen, B. and Wagle, N. 2014. 'Community-driven multiple use water services: lessons learned by the Rural Village Water Resources Management Project in Nepal'. *Water Alternatives* 7(1): 160–77 <www.water-alternatives.org/index.php/alldoc/articles/vol7/v7issue1/239-a7-1-10/file> [accessed 3 February 2014].

Ravnborg, H.M., Bustamante, R., Cissé, A., Cold-Ravnkilde, S.M., Cossio, V., Djiré, M., Funder, M., Gómez, L.I., Le, P., Mweemba, C., Nyambe, I., Paz, T., Pham, H., Rivas, R., Skielboe, T. and Yen, N.T.B. 2012. 'The challenges of local water governance: the extent, nature and intensity of water-related conflict and cooperation', *Water Policy* 14(2): 336–57. <http://dx.doi.org/10.2166/wp.2011.097>.

Renault D. 2008. 'Service oriented management and multiple uses of water in modernizing large irrigation systems', in J. Butterworth, M. Keijzer, I. Smout and F. Hagos (eds), *Multiple Use Water Services*, Proceedings of a Multiple Use Water Services (MUS) Group international symposium held in Addis Ababa, Ethiopia, 4-6 November.

Renault, D. 2010. *Multiple Uses of Water Services in Large Irrigation Systems: Auditing and planning modernization. The MASSMUS Approach.* Rome: FAO.

Renwick, M.E. 2001. 'Valuing water in multiple-use irrigation systems: irrigated agriculture and reservoir fisheries', *Irrigation & Drainage Systems* 15(2): 149–71.

Renwick, M. et al. 2007. *Multiple Use Water Services for the Poor: Assessing the State of Knowledge.* Arlington, VA: Winrock International. <http://docs.watsan.net/Downloaded_Files/PDF/WinrockInt-2007-Multiple.pdf> [accessed 5 February 2014].

Renwick, M. 2010. 'Expert Note MUS Cost-Benefit Analysis Workshop'. Leiden, February 22–25, MUS Group.

Renwick, M. 2012. 'MUS in Winrock International', in Joe Ramaru and Jurgen Hagmann (facilitators), *Workshop Documentation MUS Roundtable Workshop*, Bellagio Conference Center, Italy, 3–7 September.

Roth, D., Boelens, R. and Zwarteveen, M. (eds). 2005. *Liquid Relations: Contested Water Rights and Legal Complexity,* New Brunswick, NJ: Rutgers University Press.

Rural Village Water Resource Management Project (RVWRMP). 2008. *Guidelines for Water Use Master Plan Preparation.* Kathmandu: RVWRMP.

RWSN Executive Steering Committee. 2010. *Myths of the Rural Water Supply Sector*, RWSN Perspective No. 4, St Gallen, Switzerland: Rural Water Supply Network. <www.rural-water-supply.net/en/resources/details/226> [accessed 15 August 2013].

SADC/Danida. 2009a. 'Guidelines for local level integrated water resource management: Based on experiences from integrated water resource management demonstration projects in Malawi, Mozambique, Namibia, Swaziland, and Zambia', Pretoria: SADC/Danida and International Water Management Institute. <www.iwmi.cgiar.org/Publications/Other/PDF/Guidelines_for_local-level_integrated_water_resource_management.pdf> [accessed 3 February 2014].

SADC/Danida. 2009b. 'Lessons learnt from the integrated water resource management demonstration projects: Innovations in local level integrated water resource management in Malawi, Mozambique, Swaziland and Zambia', Pretoria: SADC/Danida Water Sector Support Programme and the International Water Management Institute.

Schouten, T. and Moriarty, P. 2003. *Community Water, Community Management: From System to Service in Rural Areas.* Rugby, UK: Practical Action Publishing <http://dx.doi.org/10.3362/9781780441061>.

Schouten, T. and Smits, S. (eds). 2014. *From Counting Infrastructure to Monitoring Services: Trends in Sustainable Water, Sanitation and Hygiene Services.* Rugby, UK: Practical Action Publishing.

Shah, T. 2007. 'Issues in reforming informal water economies of low-income countries: Examples from India and elsewhere', in Barbara van Koppen, Mark Giordano, and John Butterworth (eds), *Community-based Water Law and Water Resource Management Reform in Developing Countries. Comprehensive Assessment of Water Management in Agriculture Series 5.* Wallingford, UK: CABI Publishers.

Shah, T. 2009. *Taming the Anarchy: Groundwater governance in South Asia.* Washington, DC: RFF Press.

Shah, T. with contributions from A. Anawar, U. Amarasinghe, C.T. Hoahn, J. Mohan, F. Molle, A. Mukherji, S. Prathapar, D. Suhardiman, A. Qureshi and K. Wegerich. 2012. 'Canal irrigation conundrum: applying contingency theory to irrigation system management in India', *Highlight #25.* Anand, India: IWMI-TATA Water Policy Research. <www.iwmi.org/iwmi-tata/apm2012> [accessed 15 August 2013].

Shah, T., van Koppen, B., Merrey, D., de Lange, M. and Samad, M. 2002. 'Institutional alternatives in African smallholder irrigation: Lessons from international experience with irrigation management transfer'. *IWMI Research Report 60.* Colombo: International Water Management Institute. <http://pdf.usaid.gov/pdf_docs/PNACQ323.pdf> [accessed 3 February 2014].

Shah, T., Verma, S., Indu, R. and Hemant, P. 2010. *Asset Creation Through Employment Guarantee? Synthesis of Student Case Studies in 9 States of India.* Anand, India: International Water Management Institute.

Smits, S., van Koppen, B., Moriarty, P. and Butterworth, J. 2010. 'Multiple-use services as alternative to rural water supply services: a characterisation of the approach', *Water Alternatives* 3(1): 102–21. <http://water-alternatives.org/index.php/alldoc/articles/vol3/v3issue1/72-a3-1-6/file> [accessed 15 August 2013].

Smits, S. and Sutton, S. 2012. 'Self supply: the case for leveraging greater household investment in water supply', *Building Blocks for Sustainability Briefing Note No. 3*, The Hague: IRC International Water and Sanitation Centre. <www.waterservicesthatlast.org/media/publications/self_supply> [accessed 15 August 2013].

Smits, S., Verhoeven, J., Moriarty, P., Fonseca, C. and Lockwood, H. 2011a. 'Arrangements and costs of support to rural water service providers', *WASHCost Working Paper No. 5.* The Hague: IRC International Water and Sanitation Centre. <www.washcost.info/page/1567> [accessed 3 February 2014].

Smits, S., Atengdem, J., Darteh, B., van Koppen, B., Moriarty, P., Nyanko, K., Obuoubisa-Darko, A., Ofosu, E., Venot, J.P. and Williams, T. 2011b. *Multiple Use Water Services in Ghana Scoping Study.* Accra: International Water Management Institute, IRC International Water and Sanitation Centre and The Rockefeller Foundation. <www.musgroup.net/content/download/1328/11685/file/Report%20MUS%20Scoping%20Ghana%20IWMI%20-%20IRC.pdf> [accessed 15 August 2013].

Sokile, C.S. 2005. 'Towards improvement of institutional frameworks for intersectoral water management: the case of Mkoji subcatchment of the Great Ruaha River in the Rufiji Basin, Tanzania', PhD thesis, University of Dar-es-Salaam, Tanzania.

Sutton, S. 2004. *Self Supply: A Fresh Approach to Water for Rural Populations.* Nairobi and St Gallen: RWSN, WSP, DFID. <www.rural-water-supply.net/en/resources/details/273> [accessed 3 February 2014].

Sutton, S. 2007. 'An introduction to self-supply, putting the user first: Incremental improvements and private investment in rural water supply', *WSP Field Note, Rural Water Supply Series.* Nairobi: Water and Sanitation Program.

Sutton, S., Butterworth, J. and Mekonta, L. 2012. *A Hidden Resource: Household-led Rural Water Supply in Ethiopia.* The Hague: IRC International Water and Sanitation Centre. <www.irc.nl/page/74548> [accessed 15 August 2013]

Tanzania Social Action Fund (TASAF) (no date) [website] <www.tasaf.org> [accessed 4 January 2012].

Tanzania Water and Sanitation Network (TAWASANET). 2009. 'Out of sight and out of mind? Are marginalized communities overlooked in decision making?', *Water and Sanitation Equity Report 2009.* Dar-es-Salaam: TAWASANET. <www.wateraid.org/~/media/Publications/marginalised-communities-water-sanitation-equity-report.pdf> [accessed 3 February 2014].

Taylor, B. 2011. 'Enhancing local government accountability: where are the opportunities?', Dar-es-Salaam: Policy Forum. <www.policyforum-tz.org/files/EnhanceLocalGovernmentAccountability.pdf> [accessed 15 August 2013].

Tembo, F. 2012. 'Citizen voice and state accountability: towards theories of change that embrace contextual dynamics'. *ODI Working Paper 343.* London: Overseas Development Institute. <www.odi.org.uk/publications/6318-state-accountabilty-citizen-voice-mwananchi> [accessed 3 February 2014].

Transparency International. 2008. *Global Corruption Report 2008: Corruption in the Water Sector.* Cambridge: Transparency International and Cambridge University Press.

UN General Assembly. 2010. 'The human right to water and sanitation', Resolution 64/292. New York, NY: United Nations General Assembly.

UN Office of the High Commissioner for Human Rights (UNHCR) 2010. 'Human rights and access to safe drinking water and sanitation', Resolution A/HRC/15/L.14. Geneva: Office of the UNHCR.

UNICEF/WHO. 2011. *Drinking Water Equity, Safety and Sustainability*. Joint Monitoring Programme for Water Supply and Sanitation. <www.unicef.org/media/files/JMP_Report_DrinkingWater_2011.pdf> [accessed 4 January 2012].

United Republic of Tanzania (URT). 2009. 'National irrigation policy draft', Dar-es-Salaam: Ministry of Water and Irrigation. <www.maji.go.tz/userfiles/Irrigation%20Policy.pdf> [accessed 15 August 2013].

van der Hoek, W., Feenstra, S.G. and Konradsen, F. 2002. 'Availability of irrigation water for domestic use in Pakistan: its impact on prevalence of diarrhoea and nutritional status of children', *Journal of Health, Population, and Nutrition* 20(1): 77–84. <www.jhpn.net/index.php/jhpn/article/viewFile/125/118> [accessed 3 February 2014].

van der Schans, M.L. and Lempérière, P. 2006. *Manual: Participatory Rapid Diagnosis and Action Planning for Irrigated Agricultural Systems*. Rome: International Programme for Technology and Research in Irrigation and Drainage, International Water Management Institute, Food and Agriculture Organization of the United Nations. <ftp://ftp.fao.org/agl/iptrid/appia_manual_en.pdf> [accessed 3 February 2014].

van Houweling, E., Hall, R.P., Sakho Diop, A., Davis, J. and Seiss, M. 2012. 'The role of productive water use in women's livelihoods: evidence from rural Senegal', *Water Alternatives* 5(3): 658–77. <http://water-alternatives.org/index.php/archive-toc> [accessed 3 February 2014].

van Koppen, B. 2002. 'A gender performance indicator for irrigation: Concepts, tools, and applications', *Research Report 59*. Colombo: International Water Management Institute. <www.iwmi.cgiar.org/Publications/IWMI_Research_Reports/PDF/pub059/Report59.pdf> [accessed 3 February 2014].

van Koppen, B. 2007. 'Dispossession at the interface of community-based water law and permit systems', in Barbara van Koppen, Mark Giordano, and John Butterworth (eds), *Community-based Water Law and Water Resource Management Reform in Developing Countries. Comprehensive Assessment of Water Management in Agriculture Series 5*. Wallingford, UK: CABI Publishers.

van Koppen, B., Giordano, M. and Butterworth, J. (eds). 2007. *Comprehensive Assessment of Water Management in Agriculture Series 5*. Wallingford, UK: CABI Publishers.

van Koppen, B., Moriarty, P. and Boelee, E. 2006. 'Multiple-use water services to advance the Millennium Development Goals', IWMI Research Report 98. Colombo, Sri Lanka: International Water Management Institute, Challenge Program on Water and Food, and International Water and Sanitation Centre. <www.iwmi.cgiar.org/Publications/IWMI_Research_Reports/PDF/pub098/RR98.pdf> [accessed 21 February 2014].

van Koppen, B. and Keraita, B. 2012. *Multiple Use Water Services in Tanzania Scoping Study*, Pretoria and Dar-es-Salaam: International Water Management Institute, IRC International Water and Sanitation Centre and The Rockefeller Foundation. <www.musgroup.net/content/download/1326/11677/file/Report%20MUS%20Scoping%20Tanzania%20IWMI-IRC.pdf> [accessed 15 August 2013].

van Koppen, B. and Smits, S. 2012. *Multiple Use Water Services Scoping Study Synthesis.* Pretoria: International Water Management Institute, IRC International Water and Sanitation Centre and The Rockefeller Foundation.

van Koppen, B., Smits, S., Penning de Vries, F., Mikhail, M. and Boelee, E. 2009. *Climbing the Water Ladder: Multiple-Use Water Services for Poverty Reduction,* Technical Report 52. Delft: IRC International Water and Sanitation Centre, International Water Management Institute and CPWF. <www.musgroup. net/home/meetings_and_events/the_cpwf_mus_project/global_outputs/ global_climbing_the_water_ladder_multiple_use_water_services_for_ poverty_reduction> [accessed 5 February 2014].

van Koppen, B., van der Zaag, P., Manzungu, E., Tapela, B. and Mapedza, E. 2011. 'Roman water law in rural Africa: dispossession, discrimination and weakening state regulation?', Presented at the 13th IASC Biennial International Conference, Sustaining Commons: Sustaining Our Future, 10–14 January, Hyderabad, India. <http://iasc2011.fes.org.in/papers/ docs/1252/submission/original/1252.pdf> [accessed 15 August 2013].

van Koppen, B., van der Zaag, P., Manzungu, E. and Tapela, B. 2014. 'Roman water law in rural Africa: finishing the unfinished business of colonial dispossession', *Water International* 39(1): 49–62 <http://dx.doi.org/10.108 0/02508060.2013.863636>.

Velleman, Y. 2010. 'Social accountability: tools and mechanisms for improved urban water services', Discussion Paper, London: WaterAid. <www.wateraid.org/~/media/Publications/social-accountability-tools- mechanisms-urban-water-services.pdf> [accessed 3 February 2014].

Venot, J.-P., Andreini, M. and Pinkstaff, C.B. 2011. 'Planning and corrupting water resources development: The case of small reservoirs in Ghana', *Water Alternatives* 4(3): 399–423.

Venot, J.-P., de Fraiture, C. and Nti Acheampong, E. 2012. 'Revisiting dominant notions: a review of costs, performance and institutions of small reservoirs in Sub-Saharan Africa', *IWMI Research Report 144.* Colombo, Sri Lanka: International Water Management Institute. <http://dx.doi. org/10.5337/2012.202>.

Verma, S. 2011. *MG-NREGA Assets and Rural Water Security: Synthesis of Field Studies in Bihar, Gujarat, Kerala and Rajasthan.* Anand, India: International Water Management Institute.

Verma, S., Kurian, B., Malik, R.P.S., Shah, T. and van Koppen, B. 2011. *Multiple Use Water Services in India Scoping Study.* Anand, India: International Water Management Institute, IRC International Water and Sanitation Centre and Rockefeller Foundation.

Verma, S. and Shah, T. 2012a. 'Labor market dynamics in post-MGNREGA rural India', *Water Policy Research Highlight # 8.* Anand: IWMI-Tata Water Policy Program. <http://iwmi-tata.blogspot.in/2012/10/2012-highlight-8. html> [accessed 15 August 2013].

Verma, S. and Shah, T. 2012b. 'Beyond digging and filling holes: 42 lessons from case studies of best-performing MG-NREGA water assets', *Water Policy Research Highlight #42*. Anand: IWMI-Tata Water Policy Program. <www.iwmi.cgiar.org/iwmi-tata/PDFs/2012_Highlight-42.pdf> [accessed 15 August 2013].

WaterAid. 2006. *Citizens' Action for Water and Sanitation*, Discussion Paper, London: WaterAid.

WaterAid. 2008. *Stepping into Action: The Second Report on Citizens' Action for Accountability in Water and Sanitation*. London: WaterAid.

WaterAid Nepal. 2010. 'Research into financial and institutional structures to support the functionality and sustainability of rural hill water systems', Kathmandu: Water Aid Nepal. <www.wateraid.org/nepal> [accessed 15 August 2013].

WECS. 2005. *National Water Plan*. Kathmandu: Water and Energy Commission Secretariat, Nepal.

Women for Water (no date) [website] <http://womenforwater.org>.

WHO/UNICEF. 2013. *Progress on Sanitation and Drinking Water: 2013 Update*. Geneva: World Health Organization.

World Bank. 1998. *Demand Responsive Approaches to Community Water Supply: Moving from Policy to Practice, East and Southern Africa*. Washington, DC: World Bank.

World Bank. 2004. *Making Services Work for the Poor. World Development Report 2004*. Washington, DC and Oxford: The World Bank and Oxford University Press.

World Bank. 2011. *Accountability in Public Services in South Africa: Selected Issues*. Washington, DC: The World Bank. <http://siteresources.worldbank.org/INTSOUTHAFRICA/Resources/Accountability_in_Public_Services_in_Africa.pdf> [accessed 3 February 2014].

Water and Sanitation Program (WSP). 2010. *Water and Sewerage Services in Karachi; Citizen Report Card: Sustainable Service Delivery Improvements*. Islamabad, Pakistan: WSP. <http://docs.watsan.net/Downloaded_Files/PDF/WSP-2011-Citizen.pdf> [accessed 3 February 2014].

Yoder, R. 1983. 'Nonagricultural uses of irrigation systems: past experience and implications for planning and design', *ODI Network Paper 7*. London: Overseas Development Institute.

Yoder, R. 1994. 'Locally managed irrigation systems: essential tasks and implications for assistance, management transfer and turnover programs', *Monograph No.3*. Colombo, Sri Lanka: International Irrigation Management Institute. <http://publications.iwmi.org/pdf/H_11888.pdf> [accessed 3 February 2014].